PRAYER BOOK RENEWAL

PRAYER BOOK RENEWAL

Worship and the New Book of Common Prayer

Edited by H. Barry Evans

*with a foreword by Charles M. Guilbert
and an introduction by William S. Pregnall*

A CROSSROAD BOOK

THE SEABURY PRESS · NEW YORK

1978
The Seabury Press
815 Second Avenue
New York, N.Y. 10017

Printed in the United States of America

Library of Congress Cataloging in Publication Data

Main entry under title: Prayer book renewal.
"A crossroad book."
Bibliography: p.
1. Protestant Episcopal Church in the U. S. A.
Book of common prayer—Congresses. 2. Liturgics—Congresses. I. Evans,
Hayden Barry, 1936-
BX5945.P68   264'.03   77-16256   ISBN 0-8164-2157-9

Grateful acknowledgment is made to the following for permission to
reprint sections from copyrighted material:

Harper & Row, for Philip Rieff,
The Triumph of the Therapeutic, copyright 1966.

Harper & Row, for Mircea Eliade,
Man and the Sacred, Part 2 of *From Primitives to Zen,*
copyright 1967, 1974 by Mircea Eliade.

The Viking Press, Inc., for Joseph Campbell,
Myths to Live By, copyright 1972 by Joseph Campbell.

Fortress Press, for Eberhard Busch, *Karl Barth,* 1976.

The Liturgical Conference, for Thomas J. Talley,
"The Sacredness of Contemporary Worship," in *Worship in
the City of Man*
(Proceedings of the 27th North American Liturgical Week, 1966).

Macmillan Publishing Co., Inc., for Dietrich Bonhoeffer,
The Cost of Discipleship, 2nd ed., © SCM Press Ltd., 1959.

CONTENTS

FOREWORD

With the authorization for use of the Proposed Book of Common Prayer, virtually the whole Church has entered upon a period of study, use, and reflection. Study guides have been produced, articles have been written, and commentaries on particular rites have begun to appear. In many instances, an increased awareness of the significance of Christian worship, and its implications for Christian living, is becoming apparent.

The purpose of the essays in this book is to explore, on a profound level, some of the pastoral, theological, and liturgical implications of the Proposed Prayer Book. Written by recognized scholars in their respective fields, they were originally presented at two conferences on liturgy held at the College of Preachers in Washington, D.C.

Their publication in this book will make them readily available to many others who are engaged in the supremely important task of the renewal of the Church.

CHARLES MORTIMER GUILBERT
*Custodian of the Standard Book
of Common Prayer*

PRAYER BOOK RENEWAL

INTRODUCTION
Spirit and Implications of the New Rites

William S. Pregnall

In the summer of 1976 Barry Evans and I sent out an "Inquiry About a Conference on Liturgy" to about seven hundred persons on a mailing list of Associated Parishes, Inc. We were a little skeptical about whether enough people would want to discuss the Proposed Book of Common Prayer after General Convention's action. By late August over one hundred fifty people indicated interest, of which sixty-five said they would offer presentations! Embarrassed by riches, two conferences were held, one in mid-Advent and the other in mid-Lent, at the College of Preachers. The staffs were impressive:

ADVENT 1976

Ned Cole, Bishop
Kent Cooper, Architect
Mason Martens, Musician
James McGregor, Musician
H. Boone Porter, Liturgical Scholar
Fred W. Putnam, Bishop
Thomas J. Talley, Professor of Liturgy
Louis Weil, Professor of Liturgics

LENT 1977

Horace T. Allen, Jr., Presbyterian Liturgical Specialist
Vienna Anderson, Liturgical Artist
Janet deCoux, Sculptor
John W. Dixon, Jr., Professor of Religion and Art
Leo Malania, Coordinator for Prayer Book Revision
Leonel L. Mitchell, Professor of Liturgics
Frederick B. Wolf, Bishop
Alec Wyton, Musician

The substance of this book is the collected formal presentations of some of the above, but the heart of each conference was the process of the interaction of all these leaders among themselves and with the many talented conferees, lay and ordained, who actively participated.

Our conference concern was stated in the first letter of inquiry: "Those of us who have been especially interested in the Church's worship know that new rites are a bare beginning for the liturgical life of the Church. In fact, the rite means little unless the spirit of worship is there." The two conferences took very different courses, but each in its own way wrestled with the new rites and in so doing discovered the real adversary to be an "angel," the spirit of worship.

To capture spirit in words is difficult, if not impossible. However, my task in this introduction will be to share my own reflections on these two gatherings of concerned, excited, and significant liturgical leaders and to suggest what the conferences point to for the Episcopal Church (and larger Church). In so doing, I will not attempt to quote statements made but rather reflect on the whole within certain categories which kept surfacing in one way or another. I am aware that many other experiences beyond these two conferences shape my thoughts. I deliberately choose not to separate these out from the two conferences, for none of us lives in such a compartmentalized world. Life in abundance came into these two conferences, was offered, lifted up in thanksgiving, broken, and shared. And life came forth from these conferences feeding abundantly many other concerns and preoccupations. So it was for me and, I suspect, for most who participated. It is from this whole-of-my-life perspective that I offer these reflections.

THE SPIRIT OF WORSHIP

The present hope in our Church today is for corporate worship that will revitalize us in our individual and corporate lives as we enter the final two decades of this century. We are done with rigid, sterile formalism, whether of high or low persuasion. Nor do we any longer embrace what a friend of Urban T. Holmes called "balloons and grabass" liturgy, liturgy in which we try to conjure up meaning and transcendence in cute ways. (*Ministry and Imagination*, Seabury Press, 1976, p. 73.) We no longer trust the clergy's pear-shaped tones to pronounce absolute (and simplistic) "truth" from a high and exalted position in the pulpit, but neither do we equate signs of the Kingdom with long-haired youths strumming guitars to the accompaniment of maudlin lyrics. We are asking for something other than these two extremes. This *tertium quid* is not necessarily an Anglican *via media* between formalism and informality, for the new liturgical experience sought may at times be both formal and informal. The priest-pastor-prophet must proclaim the Word to the people gathered. The youth with guitar and contemporary song is entirely appropriate in celebrating our redemption in Christ. But sermon and music, liturgical rites and actions, must somehow touch our lives deeply, drawing them into the revitalizing presence of the transcendent God.

This revitalizing experience of worship needs to be both reverent and earthy. By reverence, I mean that worship needs to put us clearly in the presence of the holy, transcendent God. For me this hope for a holy benchmark in my ordinary day-to-day existence is not a desire for a return of theological categories or language which set up a natural-supernatural dichotomy again. Dietrich Bonhoeffer's "God is the beyond in our midst" is closer to my hope. (*Letters and Papers from Prison,* SCM Press, 1953, p. 93.) A more traditional way of saying this is that I hope for a return of a sense of the sacramental presence of God in all of life. When we experience this, our Sunday gathering in the Lord's name becomes an intense focusing of this day-to-day sacramental reality. This holy transcendence cannot be conjured up by gimmickry, but it can be blocked by inept and inadequate attention given to the drama of worship. Poor reading, poor singing, poor selection of music, poor preaching, poor ceremony do impoverish our experience of the Spirit. Thank God we cannot stop that breath of fresh breeze which "blows where it wills, and you hear the sound of it, but you do not know whence it comes or whither it goes" (John 3:8). We can't stop this presence, but we do impede our perception of the Spirit in poorly planned and poorly done liturgy. This experience of God's presence in our midst is what I need most. It is the beginning of my new life. A sense of reverence in worship is important.

Worship needs to be reverent and earthy. By earthy, I mean it is of the clay and spittle of Adam. Worship is a lifting up of my ordinary life before God. Liturgy needs to encourage, welcome, elicit my real presence. So many services I attend encourage me to be there only in part. They don't demand anything of me. No adequate silence is given during which I have time to get in touch with my genuine sinfulness before I must mouth words of confession. My confession must be more than a listing of my petty individualistic sins. I must confess the sins of the world of which I am a part, the sins so eloquently described by John Dixon later in this book. No Scripture is read with power enough to break through my deaf ears. No sermon is preached which speaks about the life of which I am a part. Prayers are read but not prayed in a way to invite my *Amen!* Bread offered is foreign to my table or any other I have known. Worship which is earthy does not miss these opportunities to engage me. The bread lifted up in thanksgiving, the bread broken, is my bread, my life for him and in him. Only when liturgy helps me be really present am I able to embrace, to appropriate, the possibilities of his real presence in a conscious, intentional way. Too long have we relied on his grace without assuming any responsibility for our response to his power working through us. Earthy liturgy engages our humanity in ways which ultimately affirm, refresh, and redeem our humanity.

Worship which is reverent and earthy needs also to be trustworthy but not monotonous. By trustworthy, I mean we need to be able to relax in rituals and ceremonies that lead us into God's presence. Anxiety and mistrust go hand-in-hand. Part of our problem with trial use was the experience of anxiety and mistrust, which diminished our sense of worship. We weren't sure where to turn next. Sometimes, even when knowing where to turn, we couldn't trust that the pages would be there, as our Green Books gradually disintegrated! As I worship in various places and talk with lay people, I am constantly reminded that anxiety over little ceremonies like kneeling or standing are roadblocks to trust. We are all ceremonialists whether we admit it or not, and we like to know the way we are to act in a given service. Simple instruction, rational explanation, and sufficient repetition all help us to trust liturgy.

Trustworthiness does not, however, necessitate boring, monotonous liturgy. In the same way that repetition is needed to build trust, so too variety is needed to avoid boredom and monotony. Certainly the proposed Prayer Book contains sufficient opportunity for variety of rite and ceremony to help us create liturgies which are not monotonous and boring.

In summary, my present hope is for corporate worship which is vital, an occasion of revitalizing my life as an individual person and as a member of society. We have passed beyond rigid formalism and careless informality. We need worship which has a profound sense of reverence for the transcendent, holy God and yet is down to earth, engaging our full humanity. Liturgy for such worship must be trustworthy but must utilize variety to avoid monotony.

IMPLICATIONS OF THE NEW BOOK

The Proposed Book of Common Prayer is both an instrument for such worship and a symbol of the Church today. As an instrument for worship, it stands in a long and noble line of Anglican Prayer Books. As its predecessors attempted to be relevant and useful instruments, so does it. The needs for corporate worship, pastoral occasion, and individual and family prayer are all met. It is a varied, rich, adaptable instrument.

But it is more. It is also a symbol. The Proposed Book of Common Prayer is a symbol of God's people in the Episcopal Church today. We are pluralistic in our social profile and in our liturgical practice. This book affirms our pluralism. We are rooted in God's revelation in Jesus Christ, but we are also children of Abraham. This book celebrates Old and New Covenants. We are sinners, but we are joyful proclaimers of the Good News. This book recognizes both. We are a people secure in our several bondages, but we are also a people who can be led on journeys into the wilderness as pilgrims. This book symbolizes us as contemporary yet rooted in tradition, as biblically orthodox disciples yet a people searching anew for the Spirit's direction and power.

As instrument and symbol, the Proposed Book of Common Prayer has significant implications for the life of the Church that uses it. I shall discuss five, some of which will be alluded to or developed more fully in the chapters that follow. The five are the nature of ministry, a sacramental life-style, the educational task, the importance of music, and the critical influence of architecture.

1. The Nature of Ministry. The Proposed Book of Common Prayer will cause us to review our understanding of ministry. This will involve an affirmation of Baptism as the sacrament which commissions us all, clergy and lay. It will challenge the sin of clericalism which separates clergy and lay people in this ministry. And it will restore the bishop to the rightful position of chief pastor and liturgical leader of the people.

Baptism is the sacrament of ministry. In Baptism we are fully joined into that body of believers who are sent out to serve. Baptism is our entrance into the paschal mystery wherein we continually die with Christ and are raised with him to new life. Baptism, not Ordination, sends us out to proclaim this Good News to others. Baptism is the beginning of our apostolic ministry. Baptism also begins our servant ministry through him who came not to be served but to serve. Ordination to holy orders is not denigrated by these affirmations. The bishop, the presbyter, and the deacon have their rightful ministries; but for them, as for lay people, the basic call and the basic commission is in Baptism.

Understanding this will alleviate that clericalism which puts the priest on a pedestal. The Proposed Book of Common Prayer is violated if one person, a priest, takes over a whole service. The people of God, the laity of God, is all of us. All have been called and incorporated into the life of the one, great high priest, Jesus Christ. All stand equally humble, yet equally worthy, in his gracious acceptance of us. This is written throughout the pages of this new book. To use it is to challenge the sin of clericalism which sets up an erroneously conceived hierarchy of favor in God's eyes. The ministry of all the laity is affirmed.

The place of lay people in leading worship is pointed out in the directions for each rite. Specific parts rightfully belong to lay persons. Lay participation can be greatly enhanced and expanded with the intelligent use of the new Prayer Book. Also, the new Prayer Book presents many alternatives for almost every rite. Careful planning is demanded. Clergy and lay people together can use the book in planning worship. (My book, *Laity and Liturgy,* Seabury Press, 1975, pp. 92–107, discusses one model for such lay participation in liturgical planning.) When lay people become involved in the planning of services regularly, their consciousness is raised in worship, their thoughts and feelings get into the service, and a new vitality enters worship which is truly of and by the whole people of God gathered. The ministry of the Church includes lay people leading and planning worship with the clergy.

The nature of ministry will be influenced by the restoration of the full and rightful place of the bishop as chief pastor and as president and celebrant of Baptism and the Eucharist. The bishop is the living symbol of the wider Church beyond congregational bounds and power structures. We need to be reminded that our priest leads us in celebration of Baptism and Eucharist as Christ's representative duly appointed and installed by our chief pastor and priest, the bishop. Much ministry has been blocked, confused, or idolized because of congregationalism. We have only to look at our urban churches in the heart of our great cities for a sad example. Congregational and presbyteral pride have often stood between them and effective, cooperative, joint ministry. Often, each dies alone as does the central city. The proposed Prayer Book rejects prideful congregationalism and calls us to the recognition that the bishop symbolizes the power and ministry of the Church far beyond the resources of any one congregation or its leader. For Christ's sake, the world needs to see the fruit of that reality.

2. *Sacramental Life-style in the Contemporary World.* As a post-Gutenberg people, we need worship which supports something more than linear, words-oriented rationality. In the sixties, youth rejected much of the Gutenberg age, and we had superficially optimistic expectations for the "greening of America." The youthful innocence which rejected our evil society and its ways, however, proved to have its own faults. The lack of any secure criteria by which they could make any rational judgments about life led many young persons to be "crazies." Lacking any secure Word of God at the heart of their being, they took off after many gods—drugs,

pleasure, and a host of religious gods as proclaimed by gurus of one ilk or another. There is a sense in which the alleged brainwashing of young disciples of the Reverand Sun Moon was set up by the families and churches which had raised bright, healthy children but provided no occasion for the Word of God to penetrate the core of their being. Many had been bombarded with religious words and practices in traditional Christian settings, but there was no effective Christian life-style offered. Christ and culture were completely out of phase or over against one another.

A sacramental life-style is undergirded by the proposed Prayer Book. The Word of God is proclaimed and supported in and through regular eucharistic worship. As a college chaplain in the mid and late sixties, I discovered that the Eucharist spoke the Word more clearly than the nonsacramental services of Morning and Evening Prayer. In exploring this with students, the universal affirmation was that the Eucharist was the Word in action. It was drama. It was taste and touch and smell oriented, as well as see and hear oriented. It was post-Gutenberg—or, if you will, pre-Gutenberg.

With the Eucharist as the center of worship, all of life can be gathered up regularly. Life is sacramental, but we have forgotten to explore the depth of our Lord's presence in the ordinary moment. The Eucharist helps us remember his presence everywhere and at all times.

Appropriate as the dichotomies of Church and world, sacred and secular, may be to communicate some truth, I am convinced that a life-style for the contemporary Christian is best served by shelving these dichotomies. We need to see all of our secular life as the sphere of the sacred. We need to see our membership as Church people, not confined to in-house church affairs but as being influential in the decisions made about our life in the world. There is a resurgence of the Church over against culture. Much of what is called evangelism and the rebirth of the Church is nothing more than the work of "Jesus cowboys" lassoing souls in the "enemy's" territory and returning them to the safe havens of narrow, sanctimonious corrals where the religious ingroup thanks God that they are not as others are. This spiritual pride was condemned by our Lord, and the proposed Prayer Book will not long support this kind of narrow piety. A fully human lifestyle is affirmed. This life-style views the world sacramentally and lives and dies with Christ in his world, regularly lifting up in faith, hope, and love the victories and defeats of this life in Eucharist.

3. The Educational Task of the Church. Obviously, this task is linked with both the ministry and life-style of God's people. Two specific implications of an educational nature need to be stated, however. First is the need for a serious adult catechumenate culminating in the Easter Vigil with Baptism or Reaffirmation of baptismal vows and the celebration of the paschal mystery. Second is the shape of Sunday morning in the parish.

A serious program of adult Christian education should reach its climax on Easter Eve. Parish life needs to be arranged so that this traditional liturgical moment becomes the celebration by the whole community of its faith in the risen Lord. As such, adults who have undergone serious study and discipline should be baptized or reaffirm their baptismal vows. Too often the Church's education program has no real connection with worship and living a sacramental Christian life-style within the paschal mystery. There is education, there is worship, and there is Christian ministry; but they remain unconnected in the thought and practice of Christians. The restoration of the Easter Eve rites provides the logical and dramatic focus for integrating all of this. To celebrate the Easter Eve rites with a mere handful of the faithful who lament, or take pride, that others are not there is a sad misuse. These rites provide an annual focus, ancient in usage, around which the whole community gathers and welcomes its new members and celebrates its new life in Christ's death and resurrection. The Roman Catholic Church is beginning to work on this educational issue. We need to do likewise.

The Sunday morning schedule is an ever-present issue for the parish. The question is posed in common parlance, "When do you have Sunday School, before or after church?" The practice most widely used is to have the teachers and children attend the first part of the service and leave before the sermon at Morning Prayer or before the Offertory at the Eucharist. Sometimes the sermon at the Eucharist is preached after the Communion, a practice that offends me and my understanding of the liturgical drama.

I would like to commend a practice which is being used in some places where the Eucharist is celebrated every Sunday as the main service. This practice recognizes the Sunday School for children as being an appropriate liturgical setting for hearing and responding to God's Word. I can conceive of the Prayers of the People occurring as the final part of any Sunday School class. Then, the children and teachers join the adult congregation for the Peace and for the liturgy of the Table. Kids like to be in on the action. They don't particularly enjoy sitting and listening to the Word part of the service.

The timing of such a proposal might look something like this:

10:00 a.m.	Children go directly to classes.	Adults gather for coffee and announcements, greeting of visitors and one another.
10:15 to 10:20		Adults move into nave for the Eucharist. Opening hymn, lessons, sermon, prayers, etc.
10:50 to 11:00		Children join adults at the Peace

11:00	Whole community celebrates Holy Communion
11:30	Dismissal

Such a plan might remove the opportunity for adult education in a class or forum setting, although there would be
nothing to prevent this before or after the above format. My
assessment is that our Sunday mornings have either not been
educationally significant for adults, or, if they have been,
worship has been terribly truncated or given secondary importance in the minds of both priest and parishioner. No one
plan will fit every congregation, but the proposed Prayer
Book with its emphasis on regular Communion of the baptized, young and old, does challenge the shape of Sunday
morning. We can no longer in good conscience dismiss our
children from the very table which, we teach them, serves
the Bread of Life.

   4. Church Music. We have all felt great frustration in using
Rite II for Eucharist and Morning Prayer, because the revision of musical settings necessarily had to wait for the revision of the texts for the rites themselves. Even when new and
good singable music is available, there remain several implications musically.
   More than anything else, music sets the mood of a service.
Therefore, we need a variety of music to sustain and promote
a variety of moods appropriate to liturgy. For too long every
Sunday has sounded the same in many churches. Seasonal
words and emphases are overridden by an insensitive selection of music and a monotonous use of choir and organ. I will
forego the temptation of railing against electronic organs and
the disastrous blanket of mediocre sameness they cast over
liturgy! The proposed Prayer Book is rich with seasonal variety and nuance. Music intelligently offered can bring out the
excitement and richness of this variety. To do so, however,

we will need to think of a variety of instruments and tunes. The tunes will need to be usable by God's people, most of whom don't read music and offer their praises with untrained voices.

Another musical implication concerns how music helps the parts of the service stand out or interrelate. The Great Thanksgiving begins with the singing (the preferred manner according to the rubric) of the *Sursum corda, Sanctus,* and *Benedictus.* This appropriately highlights what is to follow. Likewise, the singing of "Christ our Passover" highlights the Breaking of the Bread. Done poorly, it is a negative underscoring; but done simply and well, it is a beautiful use of music for dramatic emphasis.

The singing of the Psalter is another issue. The Psalms were written to be sung, but more often than not we fail to do so. The use of a cantor with congregational repetition of a simple refrain is one answer. No matter how a particular congregation decides to sing the Psalms, however, the result should be the fullest possible participation which musically offers praise to God. A choir performance which silences the people is not the answer.

A final musical issue is the use of an expanded musical base —instruments of all kinds and electronically produced music (not organ) which is adequately amplified. The Church has been slow to recognize anything but choir and organ. This will change.

5. Church Architecture. The Proposed Book of Common Prayer demands a free-standing altar table; a visible font; a credence table in the congregation; and liturgical space usable for a variety of movements, whether passing the Peace, having a wedding, or receiving Communion. This is not to say that the proposed Prayer Book is impossible to use in churches of "traditional" architecture. It is to say, however, that to do so is to miss much of the spirit of freedom and congregational participation implied by the new rites.

Our interior architecture and furniture, as much as any

other factor, has locked us in liturgically. To exchange the Peace is very difficult physically and spiritually when high-walled pews say "stay apart," "don't allow yourselves to be drawn together in that peace which passes understanding." If the Offertory procession is only an acolyte picking up a little round silver box off a shelf in the sanctuary and moving three or four feet with its contents of unreal "wafers," that obscures the offering of my life and labor to the Lord, which offering I desperately need to be lifted up and transformed within his life once offered for me. A credence table in the congregation from which my real bread and wine are taken to the altar table better imparts the meaning of what's happening.

Pews and altar rails are liturgical curses and should be removed. They are late in origin, and they need not remain. (See Marion J. Hatchett, *Sanctifying Life, Time, and Space*, Seabury Press, 1976, pp. 93, 134–35.) Movable chairs and standing to receive Communion are more ancient and practical in usage. They promote the notion of a festive gathering, a foretaste of a heavenly banquet. Sitting in rigidly placed rows and kneeling quietly at the altar rail reinforces our passivity and individualism in worship rather than our active membership in the corporate body.

The altar against the "east" wall forces the celebrant to turn his back on the people. It becomes only an altar and not a table in that position. Whereas we have too long forgotten the sacrificial aspect while sentimentalizing the family meal aspect of the Eucharist, we can no longer fail to recognize that we are involved in both sacrifice and meal. The Last Supper makes no sense without the Cross of Calvary. But the Cross of Calvary is an isolated moment, detached from my existence without the responsive act of the Lord's Supper to the command, "Do this in remembrance of me." The altar table must be free-standing, preferably in the midst of the people, not spatially or psychologically removed by distance, rood screen, or altar rails.

The Proposed Book of Common Prayer has these and

many other implications for us. The overwhelming positive response to its publication is ample testimony to the love and labor which went into its preparation, a process initiated by the 1949 General Convention a generation ago. Over 900,000 copies have been sold at the time of this writing. The Lutheran Church has adopted the new Psalter. There are reports of use by the Anglican Church in Canada and the Roman Catholic Church in France. It is hoped that the following essays will enhance our understanding of liturgy and thus our appreciation and better use of the proposed Prayer Book.

Virginia Theological Seminary
Easter Season 1977

1

THE PASTORAL IMPLEMENTATION OF LITURGICAL PRINCIPLE

Louis Weil

EDITOR'S INTRODUCTION

A concern of the conference at which this essay was presented was that a new Prayer Book is not enough. Unless worshipers experience and understand the underlying meaning, the service will simply be new words for old ideas. Louis Weil, Professor of Liturgics at Nashotah House, takes up this issue of "liturgical mentality" in the Church versus the pastoral intentions behind the proposed Prayer Book. He points out that this is a matter of concern for those who conduct worship and for those who participate in it. Professor Weil selects several key illustrations of what pastoral implementation means. First, he deals with the role of the bishop, whose liturgical and pastoral relationship to the local congregation is reasserted in these rites. Next, he points out that the context for both infant Baptism and Communion of children is the adult *believing community. He, then, discusses the principle of flexibility in the structure and music of the services, so that we make use of the appropriate manner of celebration for a variety of occasions. Finally,*

*Weil addresses the meaning of the Eucharistic Prayer and
makes the important point that it is a proclamation of the
history of salvation and a statement of Trinitarian faith,
more than a formula of consecration. These illustrations
reinforce his thesis that implementation of new services must
be rooted in a total renewal of the Church.*

The past decade has witnessed an extraordinary level of
activity within the Church in connection with the revision
and general refurbishing of our liturgical rites. It would
hardly be my purpose to underestimate the significance of
that activity or to deny my joy at the overwhelming approval
given by the recent General Convention to the fruit of all
that work. Yet it is obvious to all of us who are involved with
the pastoral implementation of these accomplishments that
although the official texts generally demonstrate a clear ac-
quaintance with the most vigorous currents of liturgical reflection in this century, nevertheless the parochial norms of
the Church give little evidence of the underlying dynamics
of the reforms. Even in parishes where the new rites have
been received with at least modest enthusiasm, these rites
have often been celebrated with a mentality dominated by
a very different liturgical understanding than that out of
which the rites were generated.

Liturgical rites signify. They express the inner mind and
heart of the Church's life. It is quite possible for us to polish
the new rites in the light of our best theological and historical
insight and then to realize that we have merely dealt with
the externals and have failed to touch the inner core, the
heart of the matter. The meanings which liturgical rites express are not limited to the verbal patterns which make up
the various prayers and other elements. Liturgical mentality
lies within the experience of the individual Christian and the
community of which he or she is a part; it springs from faith
and thus is shaped by the character of that faith. Our liturgical catechesis in the Episcopal Church has so often been

limited to an exultation over the aesthetic qualities of "our incomparable liturgy" that the relationship of liturgical acts to faith has been little discussed. The result has been an objectification of the liturgical experience as something "out there"—an essentially clerical activity which the laity gather to observe, from which they receive spiritual and aesthetic satisfaction and in which they participate in a derived sense.

The Proposed Book of Common Prayer is a victory—of sorts. It will signify an authentic victory if we recognize that the work has only just begun. The context within which a liturgical rite is celebrated is of fundamental importance in regard to the signifying power of the rite itself. The most beautiful liturgical rite, if celebrated in a deprived context, is impaired, is denied its full power to signify the underlying mystery of God in Christ. To raise this issue is to suggest a wide array of questions and problems—far more, in fact, than we could begin to look at here. In the most direct way, it poses the question of the general norms for celebration which the rites themselves presume.

The total framework of liturgical norms puts before us the ecclesial context out of which the rites have developed and which they in turn express. These norms, on the other hand, raise the previously mentioned question of liturgical mentality, since every Christian who participates in the liturgy inevitably brings to the celebration a highly personal pattern of interpretation which has been shaped through the totality of a life experience. The clergy may have all sorts of renewed intentions and attitudes at work in their implementation of a new rite, but the use of such a rite alone in no way assures that the laity will bring comparable attitudes to the celebration.

Nor is this merely a question of the renewal of the attitudes of the laity. The issue of liturgical mentality knows no clerical/lay distinction. Having been involved in theological education for fifteen years, I am particularly alert to the fact that our clergy are little able to implement new insights, because they continue to try to interpret (and often reject) the new rites and the theology they presuppose in the light of the training they received in seminary. The problem of the formation of the clergy cannot be complacently relegated to the situation of thirty or forty years ago. Candidates for holy orders come out of parishes, and the liturgical life of those parishes is itself a highly powerful conditioner of their views. Some students, no matter what is taught in class or celebrated in the seminary chapel, will go out to perpetuate the attitudes they brought with them to seminary. Further, since those attitudes often presume a liturgy which is priest-dominated, they will be little inclined to open the awareness of their people to the significance of liturgical worship as the common activity of all of God's people gathered, and to which each diverse member brings a particular charism in the expression of personal faith and a life lived in Christ.

I begin with these matters because it is for me almost impossible to speak of the pastoral implementation of the new rites without first of all taking stock of the vastness of the problem and to recognize that for such implementation to have any real significance it must be rooted in the total renewal of the Church in faith, in preaching, in teaching, and in the meaning of community for those who bear the mark of Christ. This latter question of community is itself the most basic question of all for it is the question of the nature of the Church. A great percentage of our programs of education, often with the best of intentions, has concerned itself with details of external practice or footnotes on Church history at the terrible cost of a lack of essential teaching on the meaning of the Church as the community of those who share a common life in Christ and who witness to the power of his presence among us today. The laity are starving for this basic teaching, and without it liturgical renewal is meaningless. As we develop a clear sense of the Church as the witnessing community of God's people, we are compelled to recognize that the great signs of our common life in Christ—Baptism and Eucharist—are called to express the very nature of what the Church is and to manifest that reality in the manner in which the signs are celebrated. Our stewardship of these signs requires of us choices, then, as to the character of the celebration so that it may be more than merely an externalized cultic drill but rather a welling up from the deep interior springs of faith.

Each person concerned with these questions would probably form a somewhat different list of priorities in regard to the matter of liturgical implementation, and hence my own list is inevitably personal, shaped by my own experiences and teaching during the past few years. These priorities focus, not surprisingly, around both Baptism and Eucharist and include such matters as the sacramental role of the bishop; the relation of Communion (including that of newly baptized infants) to Christian initiation; the integral structuring of liturgical rites (with special reference to the Entrance Rite); music as an intrinsic dynamic of liturgical expression rather than an aesthetic option controlled by its own distinct norms; and finally, for a Church which now officially professes that the Holy Eucharist is "the principal act of Christian worship on the Lord's Day," the significance of that principle for our understanding of the meaning of the Eucharistic Prayer. These are important questions, and I am aware that there are others of perhaps comparable importance. Yet let us begin to explore these issues as at least a way of getting into a different understanding of what it means for Christians to gather, to hear the Word, and to celebrate the Signs.

THE SACRAMENTAL ROLE OF THE BISHOP

For a Church which prides itself on the central role of the bishop in the Church's life, it is surprising how little that role has manifested itself in connection with the evangelical, catechetical, and sacramental aspects of the life of the diocese. The visitation of the bishop is usually an occasion of some importance in the parishes and missions under his jurisdiction, and yet all too often the sacramental dimension of that visitation is little more than an occasion for the Confirmation or Reception of the persons whom, presumably, the parish priest has prepared. Frequently, the bishop's visitation has not included his presiding at a celebration of the Eucharist and occasionally has not included even his preaching. The issue is not simply that of changing the type of service or the parts which the various participants take. It is true that the new rites of initiation manifestly presume that these rites will, normatively, take part within the context of the Eucharist, but we must consider a deeper question if this is not to be simply the substitution of one service for another.

The fact that the new rites presume the active involvement of the bishop in the sacramental action is a sign of renewed and deepened awareness of who the bishop is in his relation to the Church gathered. The rubrics indicate that he is "expected to preach the Word" and preside over the entire liturgical action. This signifies a potential revolution in our customary practice, so that the bishop would not be merely a visiting administrator of an ecclesiastical unit. His guardianship of the local community of faith would be given clear expression through his liturgical role. The purpose is not that the bishop should usurp all the other legitimate roles within the liturgical action but rather that he should appear in his true function as the chief liturgical officer of his diocese. This has long been asserted in theory, but it is vain if it does not take concrete expression. Unfortunately, this role of the bishop and the complementary roles of the other clerical and lay ministries is not yet a normal dimension of our liturgical practice, and the bishop continues to act in the sanctuary rather as a guest than as the chief pastor of the community. Our scarcely disguised congregationalism is here given a rather powerful expression.

Behind the rubrics of the new rites there lies a basic theological consideration: the importance of the bishop as a human symbol. The bishop is a living symbol of unity within his diocese and between the people of his diocese and those of the other dioceses whose bishops form with him the college of chief pastors of the Church. If an episcopal polity is to have any substantial meaning, we surely must begin from this traditional perspective: that communion within the Church is signified in and through the bishops. Thus, during a visitation, a very significant aspect of the Church's life is given concrete expression through the sacramental role of the bishop when he fulfills his office as principal liturgical officer. He becomes a living link between that community and all the other communities which share his pastoral guardianship. He is thus a true *pontifex,* a bridge builder, the one who in his own person binds together the diverse elements of the diocese, interpreting them to one another and drawing them into the wider fellowship of the Church at large. A significant focus for this latter role is seen in the duty of the bishop to preach on these occasions and to the best of his ability to fulfill the office of teacher and evangelist to his people.

Given the complexity of diocesan life generally, it will be impossible in most instances for the bishop to be present for Baptism at all the various parishes and missions of his diocese. The reservation of Confirmation, Reception, and Reaffirmation, and the implied reservation, when possible, of the Baptism of adult converts to those occasions when the bishop is present, emphasize the importance of the relationship of the mature Christian through the bishop to the wider Church at the time of an adult commitment. For this dimension to come more clearly into the awareness of the Church as a whole, the preparation of these candidates and the liturgical rite in which that mature commitment will find expression must be undertaken with enormous care. As we have observed, the rites themselves will accomplish little unless they are rooted in a wider and deeper ministry at all the other levels of the Church's life.

ADULTS AS NORMATIVE CANDIDATES FOR BAPTISM

The structure of the new rite of Baptism is significant: adults and older children are presented first. The rite itself thus conveys the fact that Baptism implies an adult or mature commitment to Jesus Christ. The practice of infant Baptism grows out of this essential framework—that is, the context of a believing adult community. Without such a framework, Baptism is rather more akin to superstition than sacrament. The normative pattern of Christian initiation follows upon a mature profession of faith, focuses upon Baptism in the Name of the Holy Trinity, and finds its culmination in the sharing of the Eucharist. This normative pattern for adults has for many centuries encompassed children as well, in spite of the fact that a mature profession of faith is not as yet possible for them. The Church has traditionally drawn children into the framework of its sacramental life because of the commitment of faith by parents, godparents, and the local community as a whole, who witness to their own faith at the time of an infant's Baptism, and who pledge so to raise the child that it may come in due course consciously to share God's gift of faith and to profess that faith as its own. That infants and small children for whom we feel this to be adequate justification for Baptism should also be thereby eligible to receive the Eucharist is a conclusion which only in very recent years has imposed itself upon the consciousness of both parish priests and theologians.

The history of the question reminds us that the Communion of infants at Baptism was the normal practice of the Church until the late Middle Ages. The practice fell into disuse under the weight of the general attitude of the period that the laity were not expected to be the recipients of the Eucharist except for the annual Easter Communion. In other words, the Communion of children was not judged to be inappropriate on the basis of age but rather in a context in which the laity as a whole were seen in a primarily passive role at the celebration of the liturgy. In our own day it is quite difficult to conceive an earlier situation in which the laity did not usually receive the Sacrament even when, in some cases, they attended Mass daily. The liturgical mentality of the period was so thoroughly clericalized that an annual reception of the Eucharist was considered spiritually adequate for the inferior laity. It is in this perspective that the question of the Communion of infants and children must be weighed. In such a context it was inevitable that children would cease to receive the Eucharist at the time of their Baptism and that this rupture with the first thousand years of Christian practice would be justified on the basis of their not having attained "the age of reason." A critical look at this development at least requires us to examine the presuppositions upon which it was based.

In regard to this question at the present time, the discipline varies from one diocese to the next as to the age at which a child should begin to receive the Sacrament. The decision of the bishops at the General Convention in Houston in 1970 restored in principle the ancient practice of giving the Eucharist by virtue of Baptism. The sacraments are, after all, God's action toward us. The tradition of the Anglican Communion in the maintaining of infant Baptism, in the context, of course, of a believing community which will care for the child as it matures and comes to God's gift of personal faith, should incorporate its logical complement in the gift of Communion as the great sign of spiritual nourishment. When there is adequate justification for infant Baptism, it would seem to follow that the Eucharist is the Christian's by right. Our hesitancy in this is perhaps a sign of an abiding uneasiness in regard to infant Baptism itself. Much of the Church has come in recent years to a renewed understanding of the sacraments as signs of Christ's active presence in the life of the believing community. Such an understanding should permit us to recognize that God's gift does not depend in any essential way upon our rational powers but rather upon our willingness to receive that gift in faith and to grow together toward the Father through Christ.

On this question of the Communion of infants and small children, let me say a few words on the basis of personal experience. For the past six years I have had pastoral responsibility for a group of students, wives, and children who gather with me each Sunday in the Red Chapel, a small frame building which was the original chapel of Nashotah House, built in 1844. Almost immediately after I took charge of this weekly gathering, a student informed me that his infant son would receive Communion. I knew the history of the question, but this was the first time I was faced with the pastoral aspect in our contemporary situation. My response was simply to affirm the responsibility of the parents for the appropriate guidance of the child, and the student agreed.

In six years my willingness to move along this—to me—new path has been vindicated at every turn and has, in the experience of all of us who have gathered in the Red Chapel during these years, opened up a whole deepened understanding of mutual responsibility within a Christian community. It is our firm practice now at Nashotah House for children to receive the Eucharist from the time of their Baptism. This practice has permitted me to emphasize to the parents the importance of their role at each stage of the child's development and to put aside any suggestion that *rational* understanding is the first priority in this whole issue. Who among us would pretend to *understand* the mystery of God's gift in the Eucharist? As I suggested earlier, if we are able to baptize children without such "understanding" or a capacity to make a personal profession of faith, on what conceivable grounds do we withhold the Eucharist from baptized members of the Body of Christ?

LITURGICAL STRUCTURE: TEXTS AND MUSIC

The Proposed Book of Common Prayer offers an unprecedented degree of structural flexibility. No Prayer Book of the Anglican tradition has presented the Church with such an array of options. In fact, this flexibility is so marked a characteristic of the new book that its opponents have often focused upon the diversity of options as a matter for particular attack.

I have used many of the new rites in a wide variety of pastoral situations, and I am convinced that the fear of a chaotic diversity in practice is ill-founded. What has emerged in the range of situations in which I have been involved is, in each case, a rather consistent norm appropriate to the particular character of the liturgical context. This is precisely the point. The new rites presuppose the manifest fact that there is enormous diversity among the various contexts in which a liturgy may be celebrated: the principal Sunday Eucharist in a large parish or a small rural mission or an informal home celebration with a study group, a celebration preceded by Baptism or Morning Prayer, or simply the difference in character between a celebration on a great occasion with unlimited musical resources as contrasted with a very simple Eucharist celebrated by a small group gathered in a side chapel. The difference in character between such occasions is obvious; yet if the principle holds true that authentic liturgy wells up from within the life of the community of faith (and thus concretizes itself in the spirit of that community), this suggests that not only are the occasions different but that consequently the character of the celebration must reflect that difference.

The former mentality—the objectified understanding mentioned earlier—saw the liturgical structure as virtually an absolute form. The *Gloria in excelsis* might be included or else replaced, but basically the sequence of elements reflected a relentless inevitability, no matter what the situation in which it was celebrated. Let me cite a rather extreme example which will at least make my point clear. I came from a so-called "missal parish" in which the Prayer Book Eucharist enjoyed certain traditional enrichments. On Sundays the rather elaborate sequence of materials which began the liturgy served the clear purpose of drawing, through words and music, the whole parish community into a common liturgical action. You may remember the sequence:

Opening hymn/Prayers at the foot of the altar/Collect for
Purity/Introit Psalm verse/*Kyrie*/*Gloria in excelsis*/
Collect of the Day

By this lengthy route, we arrived at the first reading.

Frankly, it never occurred to me that the Epistle was the first element of major importance after that long sequence. The liturgy was *experienced* as a long series of liturgical and musical elements. As I look back now, however, the extraordinary thing is not that this elaborate pattern took place at the principal Sunday Eucharist but rather that it took place at *every* celebration (with the exception, of course, of the omission of music), even on sleepy mornings at 6:30 A.M. before people went on to their jobs. What the flexibility of the new book offers to the Church is not the abolition of a full liturgical pattern where that is appropriate but rather the option of simpler alternatives when the character of the gathering would plead for such simplicity.

It comes down to being a question of pastoral common sense once we recognize that the essential structure of the liturgy is a thing of marvelous simplicity, which may be elaborated and enriched in accordance with available resources and the nature of the situation. We have, however, tended to start from the other end, from the pattern of a full, elaborate celebration (even in the image of a great cathedral, which can hardly be normative) and to keep this full pattern, all elements included, as the ideal pattern for liturgical worship. Last fall one of the new seminarians asked me, "Why have they left the Prayer of Humble Access out of Rite II?" I said, "You have started at the wrong end—it was never there in the first place." The student's question, however, is typical of the attitudes I have met among many people, namely, that *any* simplification robs them of this, that, or the other prayer which is particularly dear to them. Perhaps the only convincing answer to this will not be found in verbal explanation but rather in the *experience* of a diversity of pattern which authentically reflects the character of the community and the particularity of the situation. In time, such an approach, implemented with tact, will help to expand the ability of Church members to participate in different styles of celebration without judging one by the norms of another.

The question of structure relates directly to the place of music within the liturgical context. I say *within* because it is an intrinsic dynamic of the liturgy rather than an external supplement. Let me get at this point from a musical/historical perspective. Most of us have heard in concert, or perhaps even at the liturgy, some of the great Mass settings of the Renaissance or of the Baroque era. The pattern of movements is fairly standard: *Kyrie, Gloria, Credo, Sanctus, Agnus Dei.* The implied fixity of this pattern was confirmed by celebrations of the Solemn Mass in which these elements were sung, often by the choir, in what was experienced as a unified musical/liturgical package. It came as rather a surprise to me to learn that when plainsong was first giving way to polyphony in the liturgy, this pattern was apparently not of any primary significance for composers, since the earliest such liturgical music usually appears as a single item, such as a setting of the *Gloria,* and not as a complete set of related movements.

In other words, this formalized pattern of musical settings for the Eucharist is simply an expression of a very late development which has caused us to conceive a *sung* celebration in excessively fixed terms and in sharp contrast to a *said* celebration. The effect of this, since most parishes and missions have limited musical resources, is that a modest and appropriate use of music under such a situation is seldom effected, and we end up with the anomaly of a said Eucharist with hymns. There is no question that the singing of hymns is one of the most important aspects of the liturgy in the experience of clergy and laity alike; yet right at the heart of our Eucharistic Prayer there is a hymn text, the *Sanctus,* and it should be obvious that the very nature of a hymn suggests that it be *sung.* It cannot be argued that this puts too much of a musical burden on our people, for there are many settings of the *Sanctus* available which are no more difficult than most of our popular hymns.

There is no reason why music cannot be used with great flexibility in the liturgy. Some occasions suggest a rich and full use of any resources available, but simpler occasions need not be musically impoverished. A familiar setting of the *Sanctus,* or an easily sung response or acclamation, can add a whole new dimension to the participation of the faithful in even the most modest situations.

THE MEANING OF THE EUCHARISTIC PRAYER

When the new Prayer Book states that the Holy Eucharist is "the principal act of Christian worship on the Lord's Day and other major Feasts," it is not simply espousing an empty formula of the Liturgical Movement nor even merely insisting that a celebration of the Eucharist is to be preferred over other forms of liturgical service because of hallowed custom. The primacy of the Eucharist in Christian worship has a radical connection with the very nature of the Church, with what it means to *be* the Church and to witness to the events which form the central core of its very existence. Such an approach to the Eucharist—that is, an approach which sees it not merely as a form of service among various options but rather as the fleshing out of the Church's nature—suggests an understanding of the Eucharistic Prayer which focuses on its significance as a proclamation of faith rather than a formula of consecration. The question is not that the great prayer is thereby less consecratory but rather that this dimension of the prayer is placed in the wider and necessary framework of the Church's faith. The problem with approaching the Eucharistic Prayer primarily as a formula of consecration is that one is soon caught in the quagmire of problems connected with determining the "moment of consecration," and thus in dissecting the various elements which make up the prayer as a whole and consequently losing a sense of its integrity.

An analysis of the issues raised in the previous paragraph would carry us far beyond the intentions of this essay. Let it suffice simply to say that during the first several centuries of the Church's history, the Eucharistic Prayer was the great proclamation of the history of salvation in the framework of a prayer of thanksgiving addressed to God the Father. For the Christians who gathered Sunday after Sunday, generation after generation, the Eucharistic Prayer was the gathering point for the self-offering of the local community and each member of it in union with the great oblation of Christ for the redemption of the world. In this sense, the Eucharistic offering was the oblation of the whole Church, head and members, in the weekly celebration of the union of all the baptized in Christ. In the Eucharist, the implications of Baptism were made explicit, and at the heart of that action there was the great Prayer of Thanksgiving which in a very real sense expressed the essential meaning of the faith which was there being celebrated. As later generations came to ask questions about the moment at which the "Eucharistic miracle" took place, the prayer came to be splintered into a series of formulas, recited by the priest in silence and quite cut off from the participation of the community of faith.

Although the Episcopal Church has enjoyed throughout its history a Eucharistic Prayer which reflects a sense of its essential integrity, thanks to the determination of Bishop Seabury to have the Church pray according to the best liturgical knowledge of his day, the manner in which the prayer has been celebrated has often betrayed the true nature of the prayer itself. We perhaps think first of the use of bells and elevations which interrupt the flow of the prayer and which suggest that the Words of Institution somehow stand apart from the rest of the prayer as of primary importance, that is, as somehow a "formula of consecration." Yet such customs are not the only ways in which the nature of the prayer has been violated. Very often in celebrations of great simplicity, where few if any of the liturgical trappings of the High Church tradition were in evidence, the same mind-set has been suggested by the priest's recitation of the Words of Institution at a much slower pace than the other phrases of the prayer and often with a ponderous solemnity. As different as the two situations might seem, the underlying liturgical misunderstanding is the same. In both cases the Words of Institution are treated out of context, as somehow apart from the prayer as a whole, and such an attitude does violence to the very nature of the prayer.

The Eucharistic Prayer, if approached as the proclamation of the Church's Trinitarian faith, manifests a pattern of extraordinary simplicity. A dialogue between the celebrant and the people indicates that the prayer is the common prayer of the whole community under the normative presidency of a person ordained for that office. When the priest says, "Let us give thanks to the Lord our God," he is, in fact, asking the gathered faithful for an affirmation of his office in presiding over this essential action of the whole Church. The response, "It is right to give him thanks and praise," expresses liturgically this affirmation and coaction of the faithful with the priest as he continues in the proclamation of the prayer. The structure of the prayer is itself tripart, corresponding to the Trinitarian character of the prayer: thanksgiving to God the Father, the *anamnesis* or memorial of the events of salvation history focused in Jesus Christ, and the *epiclesis* or invocation of God the Holy Spirit upon the bread and wine and also upon the faithful people assembled. When we consider the great diversity which this essential structure has taken in the course of the Church's history and how local tradition and culture have expressed this underlying purpose in the theological images developed out of its own life in Christ, it is a marvel to find the splendid unity which exists among the various forms of the Eucharistic Prayer in regard to its essential shape.

The Eucharistic Prayer, whatever its particular form or tradition, is always essentially a prayer of thanksgiving addressed to God the Father. We see in this characteristic the close relation which our whole eucharistic tradition bears to the Jewish prayer patterns of praise and thanksgiving. Our Eucharistic Prayer is in its most fundamental dynamic a prayer of *thanksgiving*. God the Father is thanked, blessed, and praised for the gifts of creation and redemption. When we perceive this essential aspect of the prayer we begin to sense how serious a violation of its character results when one passage within it comes to be isolated from the rest of the prayer as a whole. All the material within the prayer that follows this initial thanksgiving is itself the content of that thanksgiving. Hence the Eucharistic Prayer of Christians moves inevitably to a focus on Jesus Christ who is the primary basis of our thanksgiving; it is through him that the gift of redemption has come; he is the one upon whom and in whom all our thanksgiving finds its meaning.

The role of the Words of Institution must be placed in this wider context. They are Christ's authorization or command to the Church to offer the thanksgiving-memorial which is taking place in that very action. The Words of Institution thus indicate the explicit relation which exists between the present action of the Church and Christ's own intention: "Do this for the remembrance of me," and this is precisely what the Church is doing. Seen in this way, the Eucharistic Prayer closely resembles the intention of the Jewish Passover: God is blessed and praised for his past gifts which are the signs of his abiding power and love. Thus the Eucharistic Prayer goes on to the listing of the events of Christ's life which are for us the signs of God's love for us and his will that all should be saved: "Recalling his death, resurrection, and ascension, we offer you these gifts." The self-offering of the Church, and of each one of us as members of it, is the means by which our action on earth is incorporated into the redemptive self-offering of Christ, that as we "faithfully receive this holy Sacrament," so we may come to serve God "in unity, constancy, and peace."

These latter phrases link us to the third underlying dynamic of the Eucharistic Prayer, the invocation of the Holy Spirit by whose presence and power the gifts of bread and wine become "for your people the Body and Blood of your Son, the holy food and drink of new and unending life in him." Our affirmation of the real presence of Christ in the Eucharist carries with it a corollary, namely, the affirmation of the real presence of the Holy Spirit as the agent of God's action in Christ. There is thus an intense interrelatedness of the various elements of the Eucharistic Prayer which enables it to serve as a proclamation of the faith by which members of the Body of Christ live. In this we see both the need that the prayer be approached in its integrity and also that the manner in which it is celebrated should correspond to that understanding. So often, in a diversity of ways, the Eucharistic Prayer is that point in the liturgy when the people become passive and the priest is left to do his own, often rather idiosyncratic routine. A recovery of the interior meaning of the prayer as the common offering of the whole Church encourages a more straightforward manner of celebration in which the congregation is more than a group of spectators waiting for the right moment to "go up for Communion" but rather a family of faith integrally related to the purpose of the prayer from the opening dialogue until the great *Amen.*

In all these examples we see the urgent need for an implementation of the new Prayer Book so deeply rooted that many of our old assumptions will be brought under judgment and that our pastoral norms will come to reflect a type of self-understanding on the part of Christians in which their celebration of the liturgy becomes a significant sign of the substance of their inner faith. If the Eucharist is the central act of Christian worship, it is because there is an inherent meaning in this action of the Church which is essential and fundamental to its life. Neither the Eucharist nor the other liturgical acts of the Church are external to that life, for their basic meaning springs out of the well of faith. It is that faith —the faith by which the Christian lives—which gives significance to the liturgy. In this perspective, pastoral norms of celebration are not a secondary concern; they are the ways in which our faith in Christ is signified.

2

CHRISTIAN INITIATION

Frederick B. Wolf

EDITOR'S INTRODUCTION

Bishop Wolf of Maine chaired the committee which drafted the rites of initiation for the Proposed Book of Common Prayer. His essay speaks from that rich experience. It begins with an analysis of the effect of our contemporary culture on the initiation rites and lists a number of anomolies and inconsistencies with which we have become entangled. Then he shows how the revisers attempted to deal with these problems by clarifying the intentions of the rites. He includes a comparative list of the purposes of Baptism and Confirmation in the past and in the new Prayer Book. Finally, Bishop Wolf turns his attention to the practical implications of the new rites for parish worship, education, ritual, and the bishop's visitation. In a relatively short space, this essay clearly identifies our problems of the past and the possibilities for renewal which lie in the future.

When we talk about Christian initiation we are talking about a single Christian rite which, by accident of history, has over the centuries been broken into three separate elements or rites: Baptism, Confirmation, and first Holy Communion.

The separation of the initiation rite into its three distinct components has been dealt with in differing ways by such scholars as Dom Gregory Dix, O.S.B., and Geoffrey Lampe.

The problems related to this separation of the initiatory rites have been exacerbated in recent years by a number of forces in the life of contemporary society and the Church. We might look at three such forces which have heightened the problems centering around Christian initiation.

THE EFFECTS OF CONTEMPORARY SOCIETY

The first force which has brought us to a reexamination of the problems of Christian initiation is the end of Christendom and the emergence of a society which is secular and pluralistic. Our traditional Anglican rites and practices have assumed a world in which the Church and the nation or society have been the same. Our rites and practices have assumed an Anglican world and an Anglican culture in which youngsters growing up will be imbued with Anglican Christianity at school, at home, at play, at work. The rites have assumed a relatively stable, immobile population where one's godparents live in the same village or town or neighborhood as one grows up; and they have assumed that one's godparents and parents are practicing Anglicans. It is an understatement to say that such a situation no longer prevails —if it ever did. In our day, most godparents have virtually no way of keeping their promises made at an infant's baptism.

A second force which has heightened the problems of Christian initiation in Anglicanism has been the emergence of a new life cycle for persons growing up in an affluent society. In the last century or a little more, the luxury of adolescence has emerged in our western, affluent world. By the time our grandparents or great-grandparents had reached the age of thirteen or fourteen, they embarked on their life's work and, shortly, on their marriage, and they might very well be dead by the time they would have been in their early thirties. In the last century this pattern of growth has been radically altered for a great many people. Adolescence, a kind of maturational deep freeze, is now a dominant factor in the development of many people in our society. Beginning as early as fifth or sixth grade and running as late as the mid-thirties and beyond, many of us are put into an educational process which defers work, and frequently marriage, to a time in life much later than that of our ancestors. We can no longer realistically treat Confirmation as a rite of passage into adult life and responsibilities.

These two forces are reflected in a third force which has done much to shape the Church's dealing with the initiatory rites. In the last two or three decades, it has become increasingly clear that adolescent or preadolescent confirmands have disappeared with apalling frequency from the life of the Church. Studies in the early fifties indicated that eight of ten young people confirmed disappeared rapidly from active membership in the Church. Many of them did not last long enough to receive first Communion on the Sunday following their Confirmation.

Under the pressure of the societal forces identified above, and of other forces, considerable confusion and inconsistency with regard to Christian initiation has surfaced in Anglican teaching and practice:

1. We have taught that two sacraments are generally necessary to salvation, Holy Baptism and the Lord's Supper; but the second is not available until a third has been received. Confirmation has thus been added by implication and practice as generally necessary for salvation.

2. We have taught, at times, that Confirmation is "ordination to the priesthood of the laity"; but it is theologically very difficult to separate that priestly vocation from membership in the priestly fellowship given in Baptism.

3. We have taught that "Confirmation is *not* 'joining' the Episcopal Church," but unconfirmed persons have not normally been counted as full, voting members of the Episcopal Church.

4. We have taught that "Confirmation is the completion of

Baptism"; but this implies an incompleteness, a deficiency, in Baptism which is very difficult to substantiate in the Book of Common Prayer.

5. We have taught that "Confirmation gives 'full' membership in the Episcopal Church"; but we have denied voting rights to confirmed persons until they reach the age of twenty-one, or of majority.

6. We have described Confirmation as a puberty rite or rite of passage; but the passage from childhood into the adult world has been so prolonged as to make it nearly impossible to determine the "right" age for Confirmation.

7. In point of fact, Confirmation has come to be regarded by many of our youngsters as graduation from Sunday School —and, far too often, from the Church itself.

8. For many young Episcopalians, their Confirmation Day was the first time they had worshiped with the rest of their parish or mission; they had had *little* services for *little* people in a *little* church—with a *little* God. Too frequently, this first visit to the *big* church was also their last.

9. In actual practice we have largely minimized the sacrament of Holy Baptism and greatly magnified Confirmation. Baptism has been administered too commonly as a private affair after the late service with only the family and close friends present. Confirmation has been administered at a festival service to which everyone turned out and for which all the brass was polished, the church painted, and the best anthems turned on.

10. Too often Holy Baptism has been administered as a kind of magical insurance against the fires of hell, with no emphasis on serious preparation, and no awareness of initiation into the Christian community. Baptism has been either a social event (a "christening") highlighted by long dresses and a cocktail party, or a perfunctory "getting the baby done."

11. Preparation for Confirmation has ranged from nothing ("The bishop's coming tomorrow; why don't you get confirmed?") to a six- or sixty-week summary of the priest's three years of seminary education.

12. Confirmation has been viewed sometimes as God's confirming or validating the individual; sometimes as the person's confirmation of God through a supposed once-in-a-lifetime act of commitment to Jesus Christ. Pastorally, it might be wiser to assume that the whole of one's life is an ongoing process of deepening commitment to our Lord.

13. Both for lay people and clergy, Confirmation has been seen as what a bishop does for a living, and their only contact with a bishop has been at one of several Confirmation services in the bishop's schedule on a given Sunday.

Beyond such confusions and inconsistencies, the Church is only now coming to an awareness that there have been far more divergent practices with regard to Christian initiation than we have commonly acknowledged. To take a single example: Confirmation by priests (albeit with a chrism consecrated by the bishop) is the norm in the Orthodox Church; it is also commonly practiced in the Roman Catholic Church. Out of our wrestlings with the problems of Christian initiation, we have become aware that the kind of deep theological grappling which has characterized the Church's thinking about the Eucharist in the last century has not yet occurred with the other great sacrament, Holy Baptism. Until we have done far more wrestling theologically with Christian initiation, we shall be caught in the muddle identified above. Certainly one of the most helpful starts in the pursuit of a well-developed theology of Christian initiation is to be found in the Supplement to Prayer Book Studies 26 by the Reverend Daniel Stevick (Church Hymnal Corporation, 1973).

PRINCIPLES OF REVISION

While it would be fulsome to discuss in detail the long process of trial, evaluation, and rewriting through which the initiation rites have gone in preparation for the Proposed Book of Common Prayer, it is important to underline certain basic considerations reflected in that process. Two such considerations stand out. First, the new rites are shaped by the conviction that Baptism bestows full membership in the Church and therefore fully bestows the sevenfold gifts of the Holy Spirit. Secondly, Confirmation rites are shaped by the conviction that Confirmation is the mature, freely determined renewal of our baptismal vows and the personal appropriation of the gifts bestowed in Baptism, with the recognition that Confirmation is one great moment in a series of lifelong moments of deepening commitment and of appropriation of the baptismal gifts. Further, it might be well to remember that the decision to admit baptized persons to the Holy Communion was a decision made independently of the revision of the Prayer Book, although it is certainly true that the decision in this regard by the House of Bishops in Houston in 1970 was precipitated in part by the revision process.

Perhaps the shifts in the new rites can be best understood by an analysis of what we have understood the rites to do and what changes in those functions are reflected in the proposed Prayer Book. Over the years we have assigned the following functions to the two rites:

Holy Baptism	*Confirmation*
Initiation into the Church	Renewal of baptismal vows
Made a child of God	Mature profession of faith
Made an inheritor of the Kingdom	Becoming an Episcopalian
Participant in Christ's death and resurrection	Bestowal of the Holy Spirit (sevenfold gifts)
Bestowal of the Holy Spirit (sealing)	Admission to Holy Communion
	"Full" membership
	Ordination to priesthood of laity
	Once-in-a-lifetime profession of faith
	Rites of passage (especially puberty)

In the Proposed Book of Common Prayer the functions of the two rites might be listed in something like the following manner:

Holy Baptism	*Confirmation*
Initiation into the Church	Renewal of baptismal vows
Made a child of God	Mature profession of faith
Made an inheritor of the Kingdom	Becoming an Episcopalian
Participant in Christ's death and resurrection	Bestowal of the Holy Spirit
Bestowal of the Holy Spirit (sealing and sevenfold gifts)	Once-in-a-lifetime profession of faith(?)
Admission to Holy Communion	Rites of passage (?)
Full membership in the Church	
Ordination to priesthood of laity	

Two of the functions listed under Confirmation require comment. "Once-in-a-lifetime profession of faith" poses serious problems from an educational and pastoral viewpoint. For many of us, the profession of faith is a lifelong process. It is certainly difficult to pinpoint, much less orchestrate, a mountaintop faith experience. Moreover, many Episcopalians, as they reach the late teens, go through a process of growing away from Church and family as part of their personal development. Frequently, if the foundations have been laid in the home, these same young people return at a later time in their lives to a full and mature and personally owned appropriation of life in the Church. At that time they may well need and value an opportunity to sacramentalize this return in the presence of the bishop. For this reason, a formula for reaffirmation of baptismal vows is incorporated in the new rite.

Similarly, "rites of passage" are difficult to locate in contemporary culture. The physiological changes from childhood to adult life continue to occur; but, as I have indicated above, the emotional, intellectual, and psychic changes to adult life do not necessarily occur at the same time and may indeed be deferred for many young people. This delayed maturation is true for some young people but not for all, so that the whole issue of rites of passage in our culture has become rather hopelessly confused. The proposed rites allow for greater flexibility in dealing with the problem of passage but by no means fully resolve the question as to when rites of passage are appropriate for a particular person.

PRACTICAL CONSIDERATIONS

Perhaps the first and most important consideration is that of restoring Holy Baptism to its rightful place as one of the two major sacraments of the Church *in practice.* Such a return to primary status would mean that, except for emergencies, Holy Baptism will be celebrated only at public services and preferably only a few times a year at major feast days such as Easter Eve, Pentecost, All Saints' Day, the First Sunday after the Epiphany, and the bishop's visitation.

Primary status for Holy Baptism will further imply careful preparation of parents, godparents, and, when appropriate, candidates for the administration of the sacrament. Such preparation will also include a well-planned rehearsal, complete with walk-through of the service, in order to familiarize them with the service so that they can participate thoughtfully and with understanding. Beyond preparation of the immediate participants, the whole parish will be involved in the celebration of the sacrament. Such preparation will include periodic public instruction, perhaps including an "instructed" Baptism. Parish preparation might well include plans for a parish party following the Baptism to celebrate the happy event.

It will be important to pay close attention to the rubrics in the new rites. The act of Baptism should be clearly visible to all those present. This may well mean relocation of the font. The actual lustration (pouring of the water) ought to be just that—lots of water, poured generously over the candidates.

Increasingly, Baptism by immersion, particularly of infants, is being restored and has much to commend it.

Whenever possible, Holy Baptism should be administered with the Holy Eucharist, bringing the two great sacraments together in restoration of the paschal mystery. When the two sacraments are celebrated at the same time, it is certainly appropriate for the first Holy Communion to be administered to the newly baptized. Whether or not infants continue to receive the Holy Communion might best be determined pastorally by priest and parents. Implicit in the new rites is the hope that no Christian will be able to remember the time when he or she did not receive the Holy Communion.

The proposed rites give new and exciting possibilities to a bishop's visitation. Both the initiatory and eucharistic rites clearly establish the bishop as the president of the liturgy of the two great sacraments. It then becomes highly desirable (and now possible) to center the bishop's visitation in the celebration of the Eucharist and Baptism, with Confirmation, Reception, and Reaffirmation in a single service. For all but very large parishes, the visitation service can include all this with a respectable sermon and appropriate festival character in a little over an hour. It might be especially important to emphasize, in our cultural setting, the pastoral importance of the bishop's visitation for those people who have lapsed from our own or other traditions and who seek now to return and reestablish themselves actively in the life of the Church. The proposed new rites, with forms for reception and reaffirmation, magnify and expand the visitation for those who are returning to the household of faith.

The proposed initiatory rites clearly enrich the pastoral and educational opportunities surrounding them. Careful preparation, rehearsal, and follow-up with those who are involved—candidates, parents, and sponsors—can be greatly enhanced. Indeed, through the use of lay catechists, the parish can become more involved in the whole process surrounding initiation.

We are only now beginning to explore the opportunities

offered. Imagination and responsible experimentation can do much to help us make the most of the opportunities the new rites offer.

As in Holy Baptism itself, the proposed initiatory rites begin more than they accomplish. It is my conviction that if we take the rites seriously, we may be brought to a radical rediscovery of the fullness of Christian life and a deepened theology of Church and Holy Baptism. Much lies ahead for us if we take Christian initiation seriously.

3

THE THEOLOGY OF EUCHARIST

Leonel L. Mitchell

EDITOR'S INTRODUCTION

This essay sets out basic theological understandings of the Eucharist. Leonel Mitchell, who is Professor of Liturgy at Notre Dame University, looks at the emergence of the Eucharist from its beginnings in the Lord's Supper and the New Testament Church. He addresses the question of what consecration does. He describes the contents of the Eucharistic Prayer, illustrating his points by reference to various forms of it in the Proposed Book of Common Prayer. He then describes the function of the entire rite and shows how, for Christians, it accomplishes what it symbolizes. This is a concise review of the origins and meanings of Eucharistic worship.

In a memorable passage in *The Shape of the Liturgy* (Dacre Press, 1945), Dom Gregory Dix wrote:

At the heart of Christianity is the eucharistic action, a thing of an absolute simplicity—the taking, blessing, breaking and giving of bread and the taking, blessing and giving of a cup of wine and water, as these were first done with their new meaning by a young Jew before and after supper with His friends on the night before He died . . . He had told His friends to do this henceforward with the new meaning "for the *anamnesis*" of Him, and they have done it always since. (pp. 743–4)

At the Last Supper Jesus took two items from the table ritual of the Jews, actions which he and his disciples had doubtless performed countless times before and which he knew they would perform many times again: the breaking of bread at the beginning of the meal and the blessing over a cup of wine at the end. He gave to them a profoundly new meaning: "This is my Body. This is my Blood. Do this for the remembrance of me."

At first the apostles took the injunction quite literally. They gathered together in the evening and ate supper. At the beginning of the meal they blessed and broke the bread, and at its conclusion they gave thanks over the cup. This was not a new ritual. It was the ritual which the observant Jew performs to the present day when he sits down with his family on Friday night to eat the Sabbath meal. What was different —radically different—was their understanding of what they were doing: "For every time you eat this bread and drink this cup, you proclaim the death of the Lord until he comes." (I Corinthians 11:26) They knew that when they celebrated the Lord's Supper, Jesus was present with them in the saving power of his death and resurrection.

In the ritual of the Passover meal the father proclaims:

In every generation let each man look on himself as if he came forth from Egypt . . .
It was not only our fathers that the Holy One, blessed be he, redeemed, but us as well did he redeem along with them . . .
Therefore we are bound to thank, praise, laud, glorify, exalt, honor, bless, extol, and adore him who performed all these miracles for our fathers and for us.

It is this same *anamnesis* which Christians celebrated in the Eucharist—exodus not from Egypt but from the house of the dead, life not in Canaan but in heaven—but the idea is the same. The mighty act which brought it all to pass, the death and resurrection of Jesus the Christ, is made present in its saving power whenever we eat that Bread and drink that Cup.

Justin Martyr, writing in about A.D. 150, said it this way:

This food we call Eucharist, of which no one is allowed to partake except one who believes that the things we teach are true, and has received the washing for forgiveness of sins, and lives as Christ handed down to us. For we do not receive these things as common bread or common drink; but as Jesus Christ our Savior being incarnate by God's word took flesh and blood for our salvation, so also we have been taught that the food consecrated by the word of prayer which comes from him, from which our flesh and blood are nourished by transformation, is the flesh and blood of that incarnate Jesus. (*First Apology,* Chapter 66)

Theology has become more sophisticated over the centuries, but we can still agree with Justin's description of what is happening. The food is consecrated—Justin's word is *eucharistetheisan* or "thanksgiven," if there is any such word in English—by the "word of prayer." A great deal of polemical ink has been spilled since the days of Justin in trying to explain exactly how and what we mean by consecration: transubstantiation, consubstantiation, virtualism, transignification, metabolism, real presence. Theologians are still having a go at it, and I wish them well. Like Justin, I am willing to let it ride with the simple words of the Gospel.

Another controversy that has grown up for us is: How does the consecration take place? By the repetition of the words of Jesus, as St. Ambrose and Martin Luther taught? Or by the invocation of the Holy Spirit, as St. Cyril, John Calvin, and Bishop Seabury taught? Most theologians today feel this is a false dilemma and a futile discussion. Justin says it is "by the word of prayer" and describes this prayer as thanksgiving. The Church does what Jesus did, it gives thanks over the bread and wine in his name and in the certainty that his promise will not fail. It is not any set formula, not even the words of Jesus, for there have been Eucharistic Prayers which did not contain them, nor any other specific part of the prayer. It is the Eucharistic Prayer as a whole which consecrates. This is not a magical rite. There are no mystic formulae which accomplish the miracle, only the prayer of the Church through Jesus Christ, in the power of the Holy Spirit.

The content of the Eucharistic Prayer has remained constant from the earliest one we possess, that described in the *Apostolic Tradition* of Hippolytus, to the present. The order of the parts has varied from time to time and place to place, and an occasional specimen turns up without one part or another, as in the Prayer of Consecration of the English Prayer Book or the Roman Canon; but the content is always basically the same:

1. We *give thanks* to God for his mighty acts in creation and redemption. In our tradition we tend to split these acts up into a series of proper prefaces. The Eastern tradition, as in Eucharistic Prayer D of the proposed Prayer Book for example, expounds all the mighty acts in order. Since the fourth century, we have been including the angelic hymn of praise, the *Sanctus,* in this section, with the congregation joining in with angels and archangels. This is all *eucharist* properly so called.

2. The *Words of Institution* usually come at the end of this section as the last of those mighty acts for which we give thanks. This position puts them out of chronological order; but since this is the Eucharist, it is a logical order leading up to giving thanks for the institution of the Lord's Supper.

3. The *anamnesis* makes the bridge from the recital of the mighty acts of God to what we are doing. Picking up on "do this for the remembrance of me," we say, as in Eucharistic Prayer B, for example:

We remember his death, we proclaim his resurrection, we await his coming in glory; and we offer our sacrifice of praise and thanksgiving to you, O Lord of all; presenting to you, from your creation, this bread and this wine.

Samuel Seabury, in the Communion order which he had printed for the clergy of Connecticut before the issuance of the first American Prayer Book had the words "which we now offer and present unto Thee" printed in capitals, following the Scottish Episcopalian usage; and in the margin of his own copy is written in longhand "Eleva." This is grammatically and logically, if not theologically, the central moment of the prayer.

4. The *epiclesis* is the invocation which accompanies the offering: "We offer you this bread and cup. Send your Holy Spirit upon them and upon us who offer them." The form in Eucharistic Prayer D goes back into at least the fourth century:

Lord, we pray that in your goodness and mercy your Holy Spirit may descend upon us, and upon these gifts, sanctifying them and showing them to be holy gifts for your holy people, . . .

Eucharistic Prayer D does something which has not previously been a part of the Anglican tradition at this point, although it has been a part of the Syrian, Roman, and Byzantine tradition as far back as we can trace them. It expands the "us" into a prayer for the Church in which the names of specific people may be mentioned, upon whom we ask that the Spirit may descend.

5. The prayer ends with *doxology*, not only so we can all join in the *Amen* which makes it our prayer but also because it is a Christian prayer, publicly offered to the Father, through the Son, in the Spirit by and in the Church.

This is what we do in a Eucharistic Prayer. We do it in all eight of the prayers provided in the new Prayer Book. Six of them do it in this order, that of the Byzantine Liturgy and the Scottish Prayer Book. Two of them (C and Form 1) follow the ancient Alexandrian and modern Roman tradition of in-

voking the Holy Spirit upon the bread and wine immediately
after the *Sanctus* and upon the communicants after the
anamnesis. But all, with different styles and emphases, do
the same thing. This is the word of prayer with which we give
thanks over the bread and wine, for the remembrance of
him.

Gregory Dix pointed out in *The Shape of the Liturgy* that
at least from the time of the same Justin Martyr, whom I
quoted earlier, the Church has used a fourfold shape of the
liturgy to follow the actions of Jesus. When the Eucharist was
separated from the meal to become what we think of as a
service, it took a form corresponding to the actions of Christ
at the last supper:

He took bread and wine	—	Offertory
He blessed them	—	Eucharistic Prayer
He broke the bread	—	Fraction
He gave them to his disciples	—	Communion

This also is what we do, as clearly and simply as we can.

We also learn from Justin, who is a real gold mine of infor-
mation, that before the Offertory there were readings from
the Old Testament and the Gospels, a sermon, common prayers, and the exchange of a kiss. It is this structure which the
Eucharist in all contemporary revisions exhibits.

We hear the Word of God read—Old Testament, Epistle,
Gospel. We respond with psalms, hymns, or canticles, or
even silent meditation after the readings. We hear the Word
broken open for us in the sermon, and we stand to pray for
one another and the world.

The kiss of peace serves to ritualize our "being in love and
charity with our neighbors," which is the required condition
for our going on to make Eucharist. This is what we mean by
what we do. This is the core of the Eucharist, in which we are
fed by the Word of God and the Body and Blood of Christ.

But if I stopped here, I would only be describing the theology of a service. We need to understand what this proclama-

tion of the mystery of the Lord's death and resurrection
means. It is this celebration which makes us Christians. Just
as it is the Exodus and its *anamnesis* in the Passover which
makes the Jews the people of Yahweh, so it is the paschal
mystery of Christ and our participation in it in Baptism and
Eucharist, the Gospel sacraments, which make us the people
of Christ. I remember many years ago reading the opening
pages of Massey Shepherd's volume, *The Worship of the
Church* (Seabury Press, 1952). It describes the persecution of
Christians in the year 304 from the Acts of St. Saturninus and
his companions. Part of it goes like this:

"Did you, contrary to the orders of the emperors, arrange for these
persons to hold an assembly?"
   "Certainly. We celebrated the Eucharist."
   "Why?"
   "Because the Eucharist cannot be abandoned. . . . As if a Christian
could exist without the Eucharist, or the Eucharist be celebrated
without a Christian! Don't you know that a Christian is constituted
by the Eucharist, and the Eucharist by a Christian? Neither avails
without the other. We celebrated our assembly right gloriously. We
always come together at the Eucharist for the reading of the Lord's
Scriptures."

There it is. We are the Body of Christ, and it is our participation in the assembly, the *synaxis* for the Eucharist, which
makes us so. When we read of the early Christians sending
Communion to those who were unable to be present for the
Eucharist we tend to think: "How nice. They are concerned
for the piety of the sick." Perhaps, but much more important
to them was that the Eucharist was the act of the Church, and
the whole Church suffered if a member was missing. Taking
Communion to the absent was as much for the strengthening
of the Church as for the devotion of the absent member.
They needed the absent ones, and so do we.
   The Eucharist is a *sacrament;* it accomplishes what it symbolizes. It proclaims that we are one Body in Christ, and it

makes us one. And that has important implications for what we do.

Associated Parishes' new booklet, *Parish Eucharist,* says this very well:

Eucharist is a way and a style of life. It is the way a parish lives: thankfully, joyfully, as a participant in the resurrected life of Christ and servant to the world. That which we have symbolized in the Liturgy gets worked out in the day-to-day life of the parish and its members. That daily life, in turn, becomes the offering of our next liturgical celebration.

Every liturgy I know has a substantial problem figuring out how to stop. Many of them seem to go on for ever, after all that is important has clearly been done. Writers have the same problem. I shall therefore close with the concluding paragraph of the earliest Eucharistic Prayer I know, that of the *Didache.*

Remember, Lord, your Church, to save it from all evil and to make it perfect by your love. Make it holy, and gather it together from the four winds into your Kingdom which you have made ready for it. For yours is the power and the glory for ever.

Let grace come and this world pass away.
Hosanna to the Son of David.
Our Lord, come! Amen.

4

THE PASCHAL MYSTERY
Special Services for
Holy Week and Easter

H. Boone Porter, Jr.

EDITOR'S INTRODUCTION

Boone Porter shows that renewed attention to the death and resurrection of Christ in the Church Year is one of the distinctive characteristics of the new Prayer Book. He cites the historical antecedents of this interest and gives the roots of the term "paschal mystery." Then, he traces the development of the paschal celebration from its beginnings in natural religion, to its reinterpretation with Old Testament events, and to its final meanings in the passion of Christ. It is a mistake, he says, to assume that the pre-Christian meanings should be discarded; they enrich the Christian interpretation and relate to our lives as human beings. Finally, Porter deals specifically with the special services for Palm Sunday, Maundy Thursday, Good Friday, and Easter Vigil. He points out that these are different from services at other times of the year, in that we reenact the original events, rather than just hear about them. Boone Porter is Editor of The Living Church. *Formerly, he was Professor of Liturgy at General Theological Seminary.*

When we speak of revised or restored liturgical rites, the special services for Holy Week and Easter may be among the first items which come to mind. We will recall that the recent reformation of Roman Catholic worship was inaugurated in the 1950s with the restoration of Holy Week. Similarly, among the new services of a number of other Churches, we find renewed attention to Holy Week and Easter. This is certainly very much the case with the Proposed Book of Common Prayer of the Episcopal Church. The presence of the substantial, distinctive, and dramatic series of rites extending from page 270 through 295 is one of the most notable differences between this book and previous editions of the Book of Common Prayer.

This distinctive emphasis is by no means limited to these special services occurring within an eight-day period. The full Easter season of fifty days has been restored, extending from the holy night of the resurrection to and including Pentecost, or Whitsunday. This season is marked by a special opening acclamation both at the Holy Eucharist and the Daily Offices, the use of *Alleluia* at various points in the services, and the special arrangement of the Sunday lectionary in this season. Appropriate chants are offered for the morning office. Throughout the year, moreover, Collects are offered for Fridays, Saturdays, and Sundays in Morning and Evening Prayer, which sustain the themes of Holy Week and Easter. The same is true of the provisions for optional votive celebrations of the Holy Eucharist on Thursdays, Fridays, and Saturdays. These themes have, of course, always been integral to Holy Baptism and the Eucharist, but it may be said that in the revised rites of the Episcopal Church, as of several other Churches, there is a newer and more vivid emphasis on the Lord's death and resurrection. This will also now be found elsewhere in the revised services, as in the celebrations of marriage and burial. We are, therefore, talking about an aspect of the revised liturgy as a whole. The attention of the present discussion, however, will be directed particularly toward Holy Week and the Great Vigil of Easter which concludes Holy Week and inaugurates the Easter season.

HOLY WEEK AND EASTER IN THE LITURGICAL MOVEMENT

Liturgists in all Churches are, of course, aware of the unique theological importance of the death and resurrection of our Lord. There have also been historical and literary factors which have encouraged emphasis on these central acts of our salvation. Ancient Christian writings related to liturgy, such as those attributed to St. Ambrose of Milan and St. Cyril of Jerusalem, are, in many cases, primarily devoted to services occurring at this special time of year. When interest in liturgical matters began to be revived in the nineteenth century, concern for the Church Year was a notable part of the revival. The poems in John Keble's *The Christian Year* were enthusiastically received by readers both in Great Britain and in America. First published in 1827, it was an important precursor of the Oxford Movement. Within Roman Catholicism, one also thinks of the research on the Church Year carried out by Abbot Prosper Guéranger. Within the present century, the basic theological research for the liturgical movement was largely carried out by German Roman Catholics and Lutherans in the 1920s and 1930s. During the domination of Hitler, there was an effort to introduce non-Christian ritual practices, and this included the secularization or paganization of various holidays. This stimulated a good deal of thought and research into the meaning and significance of seasonal observances on the part of German Christians. That seems a long time ago now, but the thought of that period bore eloquent contemporary fruit in two more recent books by the renowned German Catholic philosopher Josef Pieper. *Leisure: The Basis of Culture* (New American Library, 1964), and subsequently *In Tune With the World* (Franciscan Herald Press, 1973), are profound and stimulating examinations of the Christian use of time, with specific reference to the observance of festivals. It is indeed remarkable when any movement inspires a German professor to write two profound books, each of which is only about a hundred pages in length!

The seminal thinkers of the liturgical movement in the 1920s and 1930s also devoted great attention to the concept of "mystery," as expressed by the Greek word *mysterion* in the Greek New Testament. Such scholars brought to Christian theology their extensive background in Greek and Latin studies and their understanding of the concept of mystery as it occurred in various non-Christian ancient religions. In the New Testament, this term is especially characteristic of the Epistle to the Ephesians, where it sums up the meaning of Christ, indeed, the meaning of the whole scope of creation, redemption, and the reconstitution of all things. (See, for example, Ephesians 1:9; 3:3,4,9; 5:32.)

With this background, it is not surprising that the concept of the paschal mystery has emerged with special importance in liturgical thought in the middle of the twentieth century. This phrase is seen as expressing basic insights for the entire Christian religion, but especially for the Christian liturgy. Such concern focuses, naturally, in the paschal season itself.

WHAT IS THE PASCHAL MYSTERY?

For most English-speaking peoples, the term *paschal* is, itself, somewhat of a mystery. The word *pasch,* deriving from *pascha,* as it appears in Syriac, Greek, and Latin, was, indeed, introduced into English in late medieval times and occurs occasionally in the older English writers. The general use, however, of the noun *passover,* to translate this term in the more common English versions of the Bible, has rendered the term *pasch* unknown except to the erudite. It is helpful to have it clearly explained and stated that, in ordinary English usage, "Passover" is the name for the ancient feast in the spring, and that "paschal" is the adjective which means pertaining to the same feast.

The use of the word *mystery* as it appears in a theological context is also generally puzzling. In Greek, it denotes spiritual and transcendent realities which exceed the ordinary scope of human thought. As we have seen, it is a biblical term. In ecclesiastical Greek, *mysterion* is the common word for sacrament, but it obviously means much more than the latter term suggests in Western usage. The expression *paschal mystery* refers to our Lord's death and resurrection. It also refers to the Holy Days which celebrate this event, and the liturgical commemoration of it. Paschal mystery also refers to our own inner spiritual appropriation and understanding of the death and resurrection of our Savior, and the place of this in our spirituality. Thus, we have a symbolic concept with a variety of meanings and implications attached to it.

THE PASSOVER FEAST

The many different levels of meaning expressed in the paschal mystery can, perhaps, be thus approached by a brief survey of its historical sources. First of all, the Passover feast was certainly a spring observance, relating to fertility and the return of life to the earth after the winter. The sacrificing of new lambs and the eating of the first new greens from the garden (bitter herbs), and the offering of the first fruits of the wheat harvest, all reflect this aspect of the feast (cf. Exodus 12:1–8). The holding of the feast on the night of the first full moon after daylight begins to exceed dark in the spring reflects the concern with new life and also the ritual concern for a dramatic celebration (no doubt originally all night in duration) taking place in the magic light of the full moon. In the spring, religion does not have to look far to discover symbols. Returning birds, singing frogs, sprouting plants, blooming flowers, the different smell and feel of the air, are all symbols in search of meanings that will do justice to the new sense of the wonder and beauty of life which human beings, and perhaps even animals to some extent, experience in the spring of the year. Although the Passover was later overshadowed by various other concerns, its agricultural aspects as a feast of God the Creator remained strong throughout the biblical period. (Cf. Leviticus 23:1–14 and Numbers 28:16–25.)

This ancient feast may have been observed for centuries, or even millennia, when God called his servant Moses to lead his people out of the slavery of Egypt into their journey toward freedom. The ancient spring feast with its ceremonies already existed, but these were to some extent reinterpreted to express the historical commemoration of the national deliverance which had occurred at the time of this feast. Thus, a special historical sense was attached to the blood of the sacrificed lamb, the unleavened bread, the bitter herbs, etc. (Exodus 12:12–14, 17, 26–27, 39; 13:7–8, 14–15; Deuteronomy 16:3, 12.) New images also came to be attached to the feast, such as the column of cloud and fire which led the people through the desert and, of course, the Red Sea through which they escaped.

Such an interpenetration of agricultural and historical symbolism is not especially unnatural or surprising. It is entirely familiar to Americans, for our national agricultural Thanksgiving has also come to be understood as a thanksgiving for independence, for the life of our nation, for democracy, etc. It has also been equipped with a cult narrative associating it with the early settlement of English-speaking people in Massachusetts. There are many references throughout the Old Testament to the escape from Egypt and the wonders which accompanied it. A second layer of paschal references also grew up in the Old Testament as the prophets saw these events of old as pointing to what God would do in the future. (See, for example, Isaiah 4:5–6; 51:9–11; 63:11–14.) Later on, when the Jews were in captivity in Babylon, their deliverance from there was explicitly seen as a second Exodus.

For Christians, the meaning of the paschal feast was then again drastically reinterpreted by the passion of our Lord. He ate the Last Supper and instituted the Eucharist either at the

Passover meal or on the previous day when they were looking forward to the Passover meal. He was subsequently slain
and lay in the tomb on the sabbath day. The first day of the
new week within the Passover octave, the day when the first
fruits of the new wheat crop were offered, he rose from the
dead. (See Leviticus 23:10–11 and *Hymnal 1940*, No. 92.) Here
is the new Passover which transcends and goes beyond all
that has preceded it.

But does this render the old fertility feast or the commemoration of the escape from Egypt irrelevant? Should we say,
as pious Christian preachers sometimes do say, that Easter
really has nothing to do with flowers or butterflies or with
strange, ancient Hebrew customs but is simply about the
resurrection of Jesus Christ, no more and no less? Certainly
Christians can be irritated when rabbits and ducklings dis-
place crosses on Easter cards. On the other hand, our Lord's
death and resurrection did take place within a certain historical, seasonal, and ritual context. Apart from this context,
Christians would hardly have been able to have understood
it in the past nor would we have been able to celebrate it in
the present. After all, many revolutionaries have been ex-
ecuted in the course of history, and not a few individuals
have claimed to rise from the dead. It is because Jesus Christ
was the kind of person he was, who made himself understood
to his followers as he did, whose death and resurrection took
place within a particular setting provided by Judaism, that
we can have any understanding, however faint, of all that he
was and achieved for us. His new life was not just magic but
reflects the power of the God who is the Creator of heaven
and earth, the God who does give life to all creatures, the
God who is the Lord of history, the God who has spoken
through Holy Scripture and who is worshiped in the assemblies of his people. Similarly, the ethical, corporate, and social
implications of the resurrection are scarcely understood
when we disregard the context of the Passover as a feast of
deliverance from slavery and oppression. So it is that Christians have inherited from Jews a complicated feast with

many different layers of meaning and have added on to it their own most important final layer of meaning as this concerns the events of our salvation, as we understand them under the guidance of the Holy Spirit within the fellowship of the Church.

When we are speaking of the paschal mystery, we are speaking of a kind of observance in which this multiplicity of different layers of meaning has maximum fullness. We are speaking of a feast which (at least for the Northern hemisphere*) is betokened by even the physical sensations of our body at that time of the year. We are speaking of individual, social, cultural, and ecclesiastical inheritances to which we respond in many different parts of our being. For Christians, this is the fullest expression within time of the transcendent reality of eternity.

Particular Aspects of Holy Week and Easter

Holy Week, of course, begins with Palm Sunday, which is marked by the procession of worshipers carrying palms, willow boughs, or other suitable reeds or branches. The observance of this day does *not* center around the distribution of small blessed crosses made from folded-up bits of palm. It involves carrying long branches with which the worshipers march in parade. Among the many processions or semi-processions which may occur in the course of Christian worship, here we have something unique. Here, for the first time

---

*The applicability of all this to the Southern hemisphere is an interesting question. In fact, each culture and each part of the world offers similarities to and differences from the biblical world of Holy Scripture. Spring is vivid to North Americans, but home-killed lambs, cakes of unleavened bread made from locally grown grain, the crossing of dried-up lakes or lagoons, passing through a desert, or the immediate memory of escape from slavery may be more vivid to peoples in other parts of the world. All of us experience part of the story from purely literary accounts, and part of it from our own real-life context. Palm trees, foot-washing, gallows on a hill outside the edge of town, and a tomb hollowed out from rock are again powerful archetypal images not necessarily part of the first-hand experience of everyone.

in the year, we are literally doing something which the Bible tells us the followers of Jesus did on this particular day. This dramatic literalism inaugurates a distinctive quality of Holy Week which sets it apart from all other weeks in the year. Here again there are also profound and unconscious underlying feelings and sensations. As we are reminded in works of anthropology (for example, J. G. Frazer, *The Golden Bough*, Macmillan, 1951, Chapter X), young boys have been carrying boughs in the spring and swatting each other with them since the Stone Age! The dramatic rendering of the reading or chanting of the Passion likewise provides a direct personal experience for all concerned.

On Maundy Thursday we again perform the familiar actions of the Eucharist, but they are on this occasion seen in a somewhat different light, because this evening they are not simply our liturgical acts but are a more or less literal reenactment of what our Lord did on this particular evening. If we adopt the foot-washing as well, as many parishes are now doing, this element of actual reenactment is greatly increased.

On the next day, Good Friday, we do not literally have a crucifixion, but the distress and grief which the devout Christian worshiper experiences is certainly a genuine grief, not simply something which one has read about in a book. Again there is the dramatic reading or chanting of the Passion.

Then, on Saturday night, we enter the richest and most elaborate liturgical observance known to the Christian Church. In a remarkable series of ceremonies, we light a new light and recall God's making of light at the beginning of Creation; we follow it as the Israelites followed the pillar of fire; Baptism recalls both the Red Sea and the tomb; and the Eucharist brings to us the experience of knowing the risen Lord in the breaking of bread.

In short, during most of the year we commemorate liturgically various events of the past primarily by hearing words about them and by singing appropriate hymns or chants, saying appropriate prayers, and making our Communions. In

Holy Week, on the other hand, we act out or reenact to some extent the events themselves. This reenactment is not only spoken or sung about in words, but is seen with our eyes in the ceremonies which are carried out, heard with our ears as with the dramatic rendering of the Passion on Palm Sunday and Good Friday, and experienced with our limbs as when we walk in the procession on Palm Sunday or participate in the foot-washing on Maundy Thursday.

Not only is the manner of liturgical commemoration distinctive in this season of the year, but the method of arranging it and carrying it out has its own quality. During most seasons of the year, the officiating priest, the choir, and a very few other persons effectively lead the worship of a congregation. Each week a sermon must be composed and several suitable hymns chosen. Except when a Baptism or some comparatively unusual event is to occur, there are very few decisions to be made; and they are, on the whole, easily dealt with. For Holy Week and the Easter Vigil, on the other hand, there are a whole multitude of events to be planned, special utensils or equipment to be secured (such as boughs for Palm Sunday and the Paschal Candle), innumerable musical options, the possibility of securing instrumental accompanists, large numbers of people to be prepared as readers for the Passions and the Vigil prophecies, special decorations for the church, etc. All of this requires a considerable number of people to give their time, attention, and talent to plan for it. The priest cannot possibly do it all. Hopefully, no one will suppose the priest should! For this week, if for no other time of the year, a large percentage of the congregation must assume responsibilities for a great many things to be done and must see to it that acceptable results are achieved. It cannot be pretended that the priest will supervise all the necessary preliminary activities. In a unique way, the laity can make these rites their own.

This planning must be repeated every year, for variations and improvements will always be possible. One year it may be possible to arrange a large Palm Sunday procession on the streets together with other neighboring churches. Or (as happened for me last year) a newcomer to the congregation may bring a new but elaborate and effective plan for rendering the Passion narrative. At the Great Vigil, there may or may not be children or adults to be baptized every year. Or the lady who always decorated the Paschal Candle may have moved away. Different Readings may be chosen, with consequently different chants and prayers. And so it goes. Each year, the purpose and meaning of these rites must again be discussed and considered, and the best way to carry them out must be carefully planned. In the future, such discussion and planning will be an important Lenten activity in our parishes, and it is hoped that both clergy and people will learn a great deal from it—not just about the services but about the meaning of the paschal mystery itself. (*The Great Vigil of Easter: A Commentary* is a booklet published by the Associated Parishes especially to assist in the understanding of this climactic liturgical event.)

All this adds up to the most complicated and rich liturgical experience regularly offered within the worship of the Christian Church. The many dimensions of action, feeling, and meaning lead to rites of unique power. For those who have, year after year, experienced these rites fully and carefully carried out, it is an unforgettable experience. Even in the fall or winter, if one hears the distinctive music of the paschal season, it quickly brings gooseflesh to the skin and water to the eyes. Great chants, such as the *Exsultet,* are indeed experienced as incantations which truly do banish evil thoughts, nurture faith, and fill the heart with hope and love.

THE PASCHAL MYSTERY AND THE TRANSFORMATION OF ALL THINGS

Different levels of meaning not only act upon the worshiping individuals, but these meanings reflect upon each other. As said before, precisely because our Lord's death and resurrection occurred in the context of a certain kind of feast and a certain time of year, our understanding of it is enhanced and deepened. But the opposite is also true. The glorious truths of redemption shed back a different light on human history and, indeed, a different light upon the physical creation which surrounds us and of which we are a part. A paschal piety nurtures a catholic and humane appreciation of the beauty and the wonder of all things. For those who have repeatedly experienced the wonder of the Great Vigil of Easter, a full moon is never again a meaningless circular secular object. The smell of earth in the spring, the sound of frogs singing, and other manifestations of spring are appreciated and correctly understood as the visible and audible expressions of the imminent power of God in his world. That most basic of Christian doctrines, the Creation, which is affirmed at the beginning of the creeds and the beginning of the Bible, may appear to us all year long as something which ought to be believed and should be believed. In the paschal context, on the other hand, it can be di: ·tlv perceived and experienced as something which we know for ourselves to be true. The celebration of the mystery of creation in the Great Vigil is not simply the memory of something that occurred in the past but a reentry into it. It is a foretaste of the new creation—the recreation, the new heaven and the new earth. We are recreated, the Church is recreated. We see that the multitude of living and growing and seed-bearing things in the garden of God is to be ourselves. Here is the garden, and at the door of the empty tomb we find the Gardener, by the blood of whose cross God has been pleased to reconcile all things to himself, both things in heaven and things on earth. *Alleluia.*

5

THE WORK OF RITUALIZATION

Thomas J. Talley

EDITOR'S INTRODUCTION

Thomas Talley gives us some direction for renewal of worship through the new Prayer Book. He analyzes attempts at renewal during the past decade and looks at the way culture has influenced our ritual. He points out our tendency to measure everything—including worship—by standards of productivity; and he also attends to the loss of community in our lives and our increased tendency toward privatization. His answer to this is that we work toward the goal of ritualization in our worship—borrowing this idea from sociologists and anthropologists who study widely diverse societies. Talley identifies six characteristics of ritual: it is archaic, traditional, communitarian, ambiguous, formal, serious. These are not the terms we would normally associate with renewal, but Talley makes a convincing case that this is precisely what we need. His implied hope is that we might make the Proposed Book of Common Prayer our handbook for ritual in the best sense of that word, and he concludes by suggesting that this may help to relate religion to our world. Thomas Talley is Professor of Liturgy at General Theological Seminary.

Urban T. Holmes in an article in *Worship* ("Liturgy and Liminality," 47, 1973) suggested that the liturgical movement had come ten years too soon. Remembering that statement sends my own mind back over the past decade and more, as I reflect upon the many forces which have shaped the latest revision of the Book of Common Prayer. In fact, ten years ago I was trying to assess those forces in a paper for the Theology Institute at the Liturgical Week of that year. There were two papers, Dan O'Hanlon on "The Secularity of Christian Worship" and my own on "The Sacredness of Contemporary Worship" (published by the Liturgical Conference in *Worship in the City of Man,* 1966).

While that paper is supremely forgettable, I would like to repeat just a bit of it to show the climate of the mid-6os as perceived at that time. I hope that this is not just nostalgia but will be of use in correcting our focus for the decade to come. For better or worse, this is the way things looked to me in 1966:

It would hardly seem too much to say that the concept of the sacred is at the focus of a pastoral, liturgical, and theological crisis in the present situation of the Church. We are, or believe we will be very soon, done with most of what our fathers seemed to assume with regard to the phenomenal manifestation of the sacred. . . . No longer does one find himself caught up into "another world" in Christian worship. *They* have, as it is said, taken the mystery out, and all that is left is bathed in the garish light of intelligibility.

It all began innocently enough as an inquiry into the historical origins of our patterns and practice of worship. That quest revealed . . . that the phenomena which seemed to bear us into another dimension really did no such thing, but simply evoked a past moment of history . . . distressingly like our own; . . . a time when the Church not only seemed as concerned for politics as for religion and for culture as cult, but even to have been unable to distinguish very clearly between them. Incense, candles, vestments, even the contents of the prayers themselves are now revealed to have had their origins in an engagement with secular history, with a consequent blurring of all distinctions between secular and sacred that has left many Christians wondering where the holy went and nostalgic for the good old days of our supernatural innocence.

And parallel with this popularization of the findings of liturgical historians has come the secularization boom from the Protestant side, just when it seemed that neo-orthodoxy was beginning to restore the reformation principles eroded by liberalism. Karl Barth wrote that the doctrine of *analogia entis* was the invention of antichrist, but his student, Paul van Buren, writes *The Secular Meaning of the Gospel.* And this past year has seen the repudiation of otherly transcendence reach what must be some sort of terminal condition in the announcement [by Tom Altizer] of the demise of the Almighty.

That was how the situation looked in 1966. To no one's very great surprise, the report of God's death turned out to be no less exaggerated than that of Mark Twain's, and exaggerated, too, was the secular origin of our ritual patterns; but that did not stem the tide of demand for renewal, now not only radical but increasingly revolutionary in its aims and rhetoric. Disinclined to distinguish the New Jerusalem from the Secular City, or the last days from the Age of Aquarius, the energies of the total culture seemed bent on rushing toward an apocalyptic showdown with the sort of blessed fury and exaltation that showed promise of bringing not just Washington but all history to a standstill. But the world ended again, not with a bang but a whimper, punctuated this time by an eighteen minute gap. There is an end now to the mood of apocalyptic orgy, and some perceive a rebirth of history, not a mere resumption of it. While apologetic feints at pop liturgy are still encountered, they usually fizzle. The one-shot pseudoritual could speak only in the historical dissociation of our recent past.

THE NEED FOR RITUAL RENEWAL

It will be my thesis that our task and our experienced need now is for the sanctification of our history as a history renewed, and that this is a work of ritualization from a fresh imaginative base. It will not suffice to burn our balloons and frisbees and return to once-loved romantic distortions of Gothic patterns, even if these be "gussied up" with the occasional modernistic vesica. Nor will it help just to "try something" that, while not as redolent of glib euphoria as past experiments, would still try to get a bit more mileage out of novelty. Ritual decisions, even if they must be abandoned eventually as ill-considered, must be made for the long haul, for the coming decades if not for all the time that remains.

Such, at least, is the personal viewpoint of one rather tattered and torn Anglo-Catholic facing the use, at last, of what could have been a great liturgical document and turned out at the last to be only a deeply satisfying one, a Book of Common Prayer that, after all the false steps of the last ten years and in spite of some nagging flaws, is, nonetheless, beyond any of its predecessors, a framework within which the people of God can and should grow into a truly rich ritual life.

But given the fact that that is only a personal viewpoint, why should the Proposed Book of Common Prayer be so viewed? Why should we expect or hope or desire that the people of God will grow into a serious ritual life? The new book, more than either of its predecessors, brings to fruition the desire for flexibility and variety which motivated our first revision in 1892. Is it not one of the greatest boons of this revision that it liberates us from the narrow sameness of 1928 and allows us to go beyond ritual to refreshing variety in forms of worship and even to a large measure of spontaneous liturgical expression? Is ours a culture that can find ritual meaningful? Isn't ritual an inherently conservative force inappropriate to the aims of an opening culture?

Certainly this has been said, and much in this line of argument was represented well, and depressingly, for an old ritualist such as I, by Edward Shils in the symposium on "Ritual Behavior in Animals and Men" organized in June of 1965 by Sir Julian Huxley for the Royal Society of London. In the revised version of his paper, "Ritual and Crisis," published in *The Religious Situation: 1968* (Donald R. Cutler, editor, Beacon Press), Shils summarized prevailing opinion among intellectuals of the past century.

Ritual, . . . which in one form or another has been present in every epoch of human society has come in our own to be regarded as having no legitimate place in the economy of human life. Its name is blackened by its association with "magic," superstition, myth, religion, priestly ministrations, and submissiveness to divine authority. If ritual were only expressive, as Asian dances are thought to be, then it might have some chance of appreciation; but it instead has cognitive and moral contents of problematic associations, and on these accounts it is discredited. Cognitively, ritual speaks on behalf of cosmologies that are scientifically unacceptable; morally it involves conceptions of the sources of right and wrong that are repugnant to contemporary educated opinion. (p. 737f.)

While others besides Shils and myself might wish to take exception to such an attitude, it is quite possible to find high appreciations of ritual that might move us to line up with the prevailing opinion described by Shils. Consider, for example, the writing of Hsün-Tzu, the Chinese philosopher of the third century B.C.:

Rites rest on three bases: Heaven and earth, which are the source of all life; the ancestors, who are the source of the human race; sovereigns and teachers, who are the source of government. If there were no Heaven and earth, where would life come from? If there were no ancestors, where would the offspring come from? If there were no sovereigns and teachers, where would government come from? Should any of the three be missing, either there would be no men or men would be without peace. Hence rites are to serve Heaven on high and earth below, and to honour the ancestors and elevate the sovereigns and teachers. Herein lies the threefold basis of rites. . . . It is through rites that Heaven and earth are harmonious and sun and moon are bright, that the four seasons are ordered and the stars are on their courses, that rivers flow and that things prosper, that love and hatred are tempered and joy and anger are in keeping. They cause the lowly to be obedient and those on high to be illustrious. He who holds to the rites is never confused in the midst of multifarious change; he who deviates therefrom is lost. Rites—are they not the culmination of culture? (Quoted from Mircea Eliade, *From Primitives to Zen,* Harper & Row, 1967, p. 234f.)

Strange as such a viewpoint may be to us, we are perhaps more ready today than we would have been a generation ago to appreciate such an assertion of continuity between cosmology and civilization. Beset by ecological problems on all sides and with a future clouded by the terror of spreading nuclear capacity, it may well begin to appear to us that our habit of looking on civilization as the conquest of nature may shortly prove its hubris by success. Still, we have no slightest chance of convincing ourselves that ritual behavior alone will clean up the rivers, no matter how much we think we repent of the utilitarian technology that fouled them. Even with repentance, we are left with a fouled world that we can attempt to correct only with more technology—and with good reason, for our technology has shown itself capable of fantastic achievements, while ritual simply cannot stand up to judgment on the basis of productivity. It has no place among empirically causal instrumentalities. Some recent attempts to "create community" by moving the furniture of the sanctuary and carrying the eucharistic elements somewhat farther than formerly have proved that ritual alone is insufficient for such an end. We may wish for a world that would allow us to join Hsün-Tzu in his praise of the rites, but our own evaluation of ritual must differ somewhat from his. Indeed, it is difficult to hear his claim that the rites "cause the lowly to be obedient and those on high to be illustrious" without feeling a pang of suspicion that ritual is but a symptom of a social model that is conservative of the bad with the good, that is repressive, inflexible, and ultimately destructive of the dignity of the individual (the lofty as well as the lowly) in favor of protection of the structures of authority.

In such a reaction we can catch ourselves running up the flags of our most dearly held values, egalitarian democracy and private ownership, but behind these there lurks an even deeper privacy. Again, in *The Religious Situation: 1968,* William F. Lynch raised the question of the extent to which "we believe in the validity, the honesty, and the authenticity of public acts in any direction." In that context he presented several quotations from Philip Rieff's *The Triumph of the Therapeutic* (Harper & Row, 1966), which set forth the latter author's contention that private well-being (or at best that of the nuclear family) is in our day achieving a dominance which to a truly revolutionary extent enables, encourages, or at least includes the breaking of corporate identities and profound suspicion of all normative institutions. Three of these quotations from Rieff deserve repetition here, I believe.

Dichotomies between an ultimately meaningful and meaningless existence belong to the eras of public philosophies and communal theologies. Ecologically, this transitional civilization is becoming one vast suburbia, something like the United States, populated by divided communities of two, with perhaps two junior members caught in the middle of a private and not always civil war; in relation to these intimate, though divided communities of two, the public world is constituted as one vast stranger, who appears at inconvenient times and makes demands viewed as purely external and therefore without the power to elicit a genuine moral response. (p. 52.)

In a highly differentiated democratic culture, truly and for the first time, there arose the possibility of every man standing for himself, each at least leading a truly private life, trained to understand rather than love (or hate) his neighbor. (p. 70.)

The therapy of all therapies is not to attach oneself exclusively to any particular therapy, so that no illusion may survive of some end beyond an intensely private sense of well-being to be generated in the living of life itself. That a sense of well-being has become the end, rather than a by-product of striving after some superior communal end, announces a fundamental change of focus in the entire cast of our culture. . . . (p. 261.)

It is not difficult to hear still a ring of truth in these words, published in 1966. But they seem in many ways to be out of touch with that time, a time which had already seen the truly vast demonstration of public morality at Selma and the ritual grief of the entire nation at the first of the mad assasinations of that decade. Joseph Campbell, speaking at the Cooper Union in 1964, took note of the funeral rites of President Kennedy in terms which suggest that in such a time of crisis, ritual does bring forward the common cultural deposit of a people, even if they are unaware of that deposit, in ways that resolve the shudder of uncertainty and strengthen the sense of common identity.

That was a ritualized occasion of the greatest social necessity. The nation as a unit had suffered a shocking loss, a loss that had been shocking in depth—in a unanimous sense . . . here was an enormous nation; yet during those four days it was made a unanimous community, all of us participating in the same way, simultaneously, in a single symbolic event. To my knowledge, this was the first and only thing of its kind in peacetime that has ever given me the sense of being a member of this whole national community, engaged as a unit in the observance of a deeply significant rite. . . . The system of sentiments essential to our survival as an organic unit was effectively reactivated and evoked, emotionally and tellingly represented for and to us, during that weekend of unanimous meditation. (Reprinted in *Myths to Live By*, Viking Press, 1972, p. 53f.)

Recounting further his own meditations on the funeral cortege, the flag-draped coffin on the gun carriage, "drawn by seven clattering gray steeds with blackened hoofs, another horse prancing slowly at their side bearing an empty saddle with stirrups reversed, also with blackened hoofs and conducted by a military groom," Campbell reflects on the civilization-wide mythological themes which that rite evoked in him and adds,

Those ancient themes and legends surely were not known to many of the modern millions who, on the occasion of their dead young hero's burial, watched and heard the clattering hoofs of the seven gray steeds in the silent city and saw the noble riderless mount going by with stirrups reversed. And yet those themes and legends were not merely background; they were the presences in those military rites and their presence worked. That is my thesis. (p. 54f.)

What is the cost of the maintenance of such presences? Whatever may be said, and much can and should be said, about the archetypal quality of our most potent symbols and their availability as a dimension of human psychic life itself, ritual is a tradition and traditions can be lost. We see daily the attempts of the American Indian to recover threatened traditional ritual patterns. In a paper read at the College of Preachers last year, Patrick Sullivan quoted the words of Elk Head to the sage Black Elk regarding the sacred pipe and the sacred traditions of the Ogala Sioux. Elk Head said that the pipe "must be handed down—that their people will live for as long as the rites are known and the pipe is used. But as soon as the sacred pipe is forgotten the people will be without a center and they will perish." ("Ritual: Attending to the World," *Anglican Theological Review,* June 1975, p. 21.) And in that same context, Sullivan repeated Eliade's quotation from the Berndts' study of *The First Australians:*

A camp without ceremonies, where moonlit evenings are silent, or broken only by the mutterings of the card players or a sudden burst of quarreling, is a camp where the people's zest for living has been lost or diverted into other or less satisfying channels. Where sacred ritual has been allowed to lapse, people no longer maintain conscious contact with their own traditions and background: and once this ritual link has been broken, the whole course of their lives must reflect the change. (Quoted from Mircea Eliade, *Australian Religions,* Cornell University Press, 1973, p. 65.)

With that rather chilling image we are brought back to Rieff's threat of a coming dissolution of society into sophisticated units of self-fulfillment, and we might suffer the suggestion that the fundamental constitutive work of any society is the maintenance of its ritual life. If there is any concern among us that these days too many merely close their windows against the noise of rape and murder in the street outside just because they don't want to get involved, then we might do worse than to consider seriously with ourselves what an ethic based on self-fulfillment has earned us and whether we are watching a dream of egalitarian society dissolve into a vast desert crowded with benign and pleasant lonelinesses.

Is the alternative a highly authoritarian and ritually structured social model of the sort that would impose restrictive status distinctions just to relieve the blandness of the social physiognomy? No, not for just that; but to forge a national identity where there is one no longer, a ritual life which is restrictive of individual freedom is highly effective in building a sense of common purpose. If such a solution seems unattractive to us, we should recall that it seemed unattractive also to the freed-up fun-lovers of the Weimar Republic. And there lies the other face of terror. No modern state has demonstrated as did the Germany of National Socialism the power inherent in ritual. Without benefit of long tradition, Hitler's ritual-smiths were able very quickly to forge texts, ceremonial patterns, vestments, and the rest to articulate a resurgent national mythology of Valhallan grandeur and power. Ritual, even when created out of whole cloth, works —and for any employer. Yet, it works not by any empirical causality but by making values public, and values come by faith. It was not ritual that made Hitler's extravanganzas satanic, any more than it was music. But its success for him points to the danger of a failure of public identity with its creation of a ritual vacuum.

That, however, does not resolve our difficulty. The question remains: Is not ritual at its best inherently authoritarian, regressive, hierarchically antiegalitarian, etc.? While the answer is, "no," it could be misleading to say so thus simply, for the question is ill-posed. A better response to the question would be to give an extensive and exhaustive survey of the findings and studies of historians of religion and cultural anthropologists who in recent years have made such strides in refining our understanding of ritual. That, however, would be beyond our present scope and certainly beyond my present competence. What I would like to do is consider some characteristics of religious ritual as I understand it, in the hope that this will put us in touch with at least a few of the concepts of a few writers in the field today and equip us to some degree to address more effectively our ambivalence toward ritual.

THE NATURE OF RELIGIOUS RITUAL

First, religious ritual is *archaic* and to that extent is authoritative—something quite different from authoritarian. The Greek *arche* has that familiar double meaning of rule and beginning, which is not evident in any single English word that I know except perhaps, authority; and for contemporary culture that word is suspect. *Principium* has something of the same double value in Latin and can mean beginning, founder, leader, principle, etc. What is common in all this is the conviction that creation is a divine act and that order is rooted in it. Religious ritual is a mode of relation to the power of our origin, the ritual itself being ordered by the authority who ordered the world. It is not just something we do in obedience to authoritarian clout; it is doing the-way-the-world-is. To rest on the Sabbath is not just obedience to the fourth commandment; it is acceptance of the temporal structure of the world. God's Sabbath rest is imprinted on creation itself. This is why so much of archaic ritual is cosmogonic. Even when the ritual is redemptive, drawing its authority from a divine act within history, it is still participation in the creative act which separates cosmos from chaos. There are, indeed, instances of cosmogonic myths which begin with the divine figure's descent to earth and the instruction of men, making no attempt to account for the earth or the presence of men on it. What is involved here is simply the recognition that just any sort of existence is no existence at all. The ritual charter which creates a people and establishes its relation to the heaven and the earth is a ritual of creation by which the founding of the world is celebrated and accomplished. Therefore, both because of its power and because of its primordial reference, the ritual occurs *en arche,* or—in Eliade's favorite phrase—*in illo tempore.* Ritual is, then, archaic.

Second, it is *traditional.* It is passed from generation to generation in order to maintain continuity with the *arche* of its foundation, a continuity for the sake of which the ritual is taken to be changeless. This must be qualified, however. The ritual does not merely reach back to its primordial authority but makes that authority present; it makes actual what it celebrates. For this reason, changes that occur in peripheral aspects of the ritual come themselves to be invested with something of the original authority. While to the eye of the critical historian vast development is visible, at each moment of that development the participants in the ritual will view its performance as a repetition of what has always been done, and will—to the dismay of liturgical historians—explain the most minor practical details in allegorical terms which express the continuity of the rite with its author. The complex dynamic of tradition is that repetition itself invests the ritual with the property of continuity, and continuity with its authority makes the rite authoritative in the precise form in which it is repeated. To knit times into a unity is one of the chief functions of ritual, and this comes through repetition experienced as tradition. Change must come, whether through inadvertance or loving elaboration or the radical shock of reformation. Change through inadvertance or elaboration will usually be modestly unnoticed until it has itself become a dimension of the tradition. Deliberate reform must show itself conscious of and faithful to the continuity of the tradition and must seek to enhance that tradition. Novelty in and of itself is suspect, if not overtly impious.

Third, ritual is *communitarian.* While individual ritual patterns are not unknown, they are spin-offs from an inherently societal pattern. (Private recitation of the Office is a classic example, which can be duplicated in other cultures.) The communitarian aspect of ritual is inherent in tradition. Like that continuity, it speaks to the human need to resolve difference in the experience of unity; and to perform the ritual *munus* with others of different races, sexes, secular status, ages, nationalities, and cultures is to touch the foundation of common humanity, that in each of us which is *imago Dei.* If what was said above of the archaic quality of religious ritual reflected a line of thought that we associate especially with the work of Mircea Eliade, it would be irresponsible even to raise this matter of ritual community without acknowledging the contribution of Victor Turner to our understanding. Turner's work has been especially valuable in pointing to the social bonding which he calls by the Latin *communitas,* in order to avoid the spatial signification of "community" in common parlance.

To understand Turner's conception of *communitas,* we must remember that his distinction between structure and anti-structure takes its beginning from van Gennep's description of rites of passage, an analysis which notes two movements, separation from the previous status structure (e. g., childhood) and incorporation into a new status structure (adulthood). Between these is the *limen* or threshold where one belongs to no status structure at all, and it is here that Turner has focused his attention. At that threshold, status structure gives way to liminal anti-structure in which the initiates, stripped of all individuating distinctions, discover what is truly common in humanity and experience the unity that Turner designates *communitas.* Something of that same liminality is found in all religious ritual and is, for Turner, the locus of encounter with transcendence. Before this transcendence, where no distinctions of status obtain (for in Christ there is neither Jew nor Greek, . . .), what binds *communitas* is that in each of us which is *imago Dei;* and it is this which is the foundation of all human association, secular as well as sacred, and gives the imperative to all society. Ritual *communitas* is radically egalitarian, for it celebrates the ultimate homogeneity of the human condition.

Fourth, religious ritual communicates its content in *ambi-*

guity. What comes forward at the threshold is that world of value which cannot be institutionalized because it is transcendent and which, because it cannot be institutionalized, remains ambiguous but with an ambiguity which opens and releases the imagination, leading it beyond barren utility. As Turner has put it, "the liminal, and the ritual which guards it, are proofs of the existence of powers antithetical to those generating and maintaining 'profane' structures of all types, proofs that man does not live by bread alone." ("Passages, Margins, and Poverty: Religious Symbols of Communitas," *Worship,* 46, 1972, p. 391.)

The assignment of meaning is inevitable in symbolic communication, but ritual is not concerned with univocal signification. The Cross is a sign of hope and testimony to God's love, because it is an instrument of degradation. This sort of paradox, and the more fundamental ambiguity to which it points, frustrates every attempt to plug our liminal ritual into secular structures. To those structures (yes, to the world, as the Fourth Gospel speaks of it), sacred ritual is irrelevant, gloriously and transcendently irrelevant—if by relevance we mean anything easier than scandal and foolishness.

Still, those secular structures must exist and must remain sensitively human; and the perception of the deepest human values must be constantly transmitted to those structures from that liminal *communitas* in which that perception is generated. Such a liminal *communitas,* however, is frail and must accept some structure to sustain its perceptions. This is the function of ritual. Therefore:

Fifth, religious ritual (and all ritual) is *formal.* That is to say, the normal balance between content and form, between what is said and the way in which it is said, is in ritual skewed in favor of high articulation of the latter, a concomitant of the ambiguity of content. Such formality is no accident, nor is it a sign of decay; but it simply belongs to the nature of ritual. Here highly specific patterns of posture, gesture, speech cadence, and intonation present a content which is symbolic, richly ambiguous, and multivalent. When attempts are made through the use of commentators during the ritual to "explain" (that is, to exhaust) the symbolic content, the ritual ceases to function as such. Likewise, when attempts are made to "create rituals" to express a specific content, the balance of form to content gives us a ceremony which can be expressive but remains superficial. Resistance to formality is most often rooted in what James Hitchcock calls, "the fallacy of explicitness, ... the assumption that a symbol or an experience cannot be meaningful unless its meaning can be articulated verbally and coherently." (*The Recovery of the Sacred,* The Seabury Press, 1974, p. 166.)

Finally, religious ritual is *serious.* Those who cannot take joy seriously may find this a gloomy observation and so may try to make worship fun or cute or something else inappropriate. The fact remains that ritual in general and religious ritual in particular is concerned with life in its seriousness and, especially for us Christians, with a serious experience of joy. Ritual is a life-and-death matter because it is a matter of Death and Life.

Many of us will remain uncomfortable with ritual, there being diversities of gifts; but I hope there will be many who will respond creatively, responsibly and seriously to the task of ritualization presented to the Church with the Proposed Book of Common Prayer. Neither old rigidities nor silly, "gee-whiz," pop rebellions against them will contribute very much. I must say that I take a critical understanding of liturgical history to be a fundamental requirement for the work of ritualization. But I hope that I have at least managed to suggest that we might attend as well to those social scientists who show us the power of ritual in humanity as a whole, for such studies can be important reinforcement for us in a time that has little or no consciousness of its need for ritual. Without their witness, we might well forget for what purpose and to what end we perform the rites; we might forget that we do this for the life of the world.

6

LITURGY AND CHRISTIAN FORMATION
Principles of Prayer Book Revision and the Ordination of Women

John W. Dixon, Jr.

EDITOR'S INTRODUCTION

John Dixon is a layman of the Episcopal Church and Professor of Art and Religion at the University of North Carolina. His essay extends Professor Talley's comments on ritual, relying on his knowledge of arts and human sciences. Based upon his understanding of the way in which liturgy forms personality, Dixon deals with the principles of Prayer Book revision and its quality in two illustrative cases, the Confirmation rite and Confession of Sin. He is critical of the way in which these issues were dealt with by the Church, but his primary purpose is to probe into deeper concerns about the true meaning and function of liturgy. Having laid this foundation, he turns his attention to the effect on our liturgical life of the ordination of women. In this case, he believes that equality of women as leaders of worship may help us recover a deeper understanding of complete humanity. Although his illustrations may be controversial, his task is to try to recover

*the full power of the liturgy for the Church and for the
world.*

I have a friend and colleague who used to justify causing
a ruckus in pursuit of some good cause by saying, "Before
there can be healing, the waters must be stirred." I could
never convince him that nothing in the story gave him prec-
edent or authority for stirring the waters himself, and I am
afraid his stirring did not do much healing.

Somewhat chastened by his example, I approach the task
of stirring the waters fully aware that if I am the stirrer, the
waters will not contain much healing power; and I have the
further responsibility of doing what I can to provide the
means for healing. I ask you, therefore, to bear with me for
the stirring I undoubtedly intend to do, in hopes that together we can find the power to heal.

Before I can deal with the ordination of women, it is necessary to set out a good deal more about what liturgy is, what
makes it work, and what is wrong with the way the revision
of our liturgy has been undertaken. To get there I want to
examine in some detail two typical cases: the treatment of
Confirmation and the prayer of Confession. I choose these as
indicating the procedures and the reasoning that seem so
clearly to inhibit the proper kind of liturgical work.

THE FUNCTION OF LITURGY
AND THE CONFIRMATION RITE

Actually, I am not concerned with the Confirmation service itself, which seems harmless enough. What does concern
me is what I feel constrained to call the destruction of Confirmation by the admission of unconfirmed children to full participation in the Eucharist. It is here we can see the nature
of present liturgical thinking at its clearest.

The question is: Why was this done? At a parish meeting
I heard a young mother say, with some asperity, "If Commu-

nion is the nourishment of the Christian life, the whole family ought to participate." She is an intelligent and serious person but untrained in both theology and symbolism, so I could shrug off her opinion were it not for the fact that the people responsible for the action seemed to have been thinking exactly the same way. This bears close examination.

In the first place, it is a theological *argument,* and it is in no way clear to me that theological argument is the determinative factor in a situation such as this. We have for a long time assumed that theology is the ultimately controlling discipline in the life of the Church, but there is no reason to think it should be. There is no theological argument in the Old Testament. There is some in the New Testament but always subordinate to something else. Why do we make this grant of authority to argument?

In the second place, it is bad theology or at least bad Anglican theology. This action surrenders a central act of the faith to a thoroughly low church Protestant interpretation—that the Eucharist is a meal. The Anglican doctrine on this matter, what I would prefer to call catholic doctrine, is that the Eucharist is both meal and sacrifice. This is dramatized in the best architectural tradition which ensures that the altar is simultaneously altar and table, the place of sacrifice and the place of the meal.

Far more important than theology in a problem of this kind is anthropology and psychology; even, in a special sense of the word, sociology.

What sociology and psychology tell us is that the most serious problem of the young today—and this means also of the adults they grow up to be—is what the jargon calls "identity crisis." They drift without identity and without purpose, because identity is essential to purpose. Lacking identity, lacking a true self, they drift into some movement or other that can provide a substitute self. Or they flee from the emptiness of personality into the obliteration of drugs or sex. Or they seek to blend into the undifferentiated unity of things.

What anthropology tells us is that every reasonably successful society has carefully developed rites of passage, initiation ceremonies that make the transition from one stage of life to another. At their best, these ceremonials do not simply accent the passage. They set out in the most vivid and effective symbolic drama possible the essentials of the stage the initiate is about to enter. The purpose of the ritual, the liturgy, is to set out the nature of the human, to give initiates the identity and the place that belongs to them.

"Rites of passage" or "puberty rites" are not unwarranted intrusions into the growth of an established personality. A rite of passage is not simply a ceremony marking a change to be left to the choice of the initiate. It is a setting out of the state to which the initiate is being introduced in a ceremony that by its energy *informs* the initiate to that state.

The success of this process does not depend on the particular understanding of the human; established by the ritual, the process itself determines the success. But obviously it matters and it matters a great deal what kind of identity, what kind of character and personality is established by the corporate rituals. It is not a matter of an established personality participating in the liturgy. It is the liturgy (the whole and not just the initiation rites) that establishes the personality. That is the function of liturgy.

The Confirmation liturgy was one of the few rites of passage left in our culture, a culture which has either weakened or abolished nearly every true liturgy. The Confirmation liturgy was a true admission to adulthood, however little it may have shaped the sense of what an adult is. But now the child is casually admitted to a truncated liturgy. The *meal* a child can participate in and even grasp with some understanding. The *sacrifice* is beyond the child, and it is not a child's role to participate in sacrifice. That is for the adult.

We can do things we do not understand, and as long as the doing, the acts, are presented in the proper dramatic, psychological order, they are implanted in the consciousness. But what is now left to be done? The act has been extracted from Confirmation because of a theological argument, thus

making argument, not act, primary. The act gone, there is
nothing left to confirm at Confirmation but argument, which
is thin gruel indeed to nourish a life.

By becoming primary, theological argument has lost its
true function, which is always to serve liturgy and the moral
life. It is helpless before the very problem it asserted in this
case; the young mother who called the Eucharist a meal
could not have said half an intelligent sentence on how the
Eucharist nourishes us. But, in her inexperience, she is no
worse off than theologians who can do no better as long as
they assign primacy to logical argument. The source of liturgy is not argument but drama, anthropology, and psychology—which is to say liturgy itself. The Eucharist nourishes us
because it implants the Christ image into our very nervous
system, because it shapes our flesh and acts. In the great
words of the sacrifice: ". . . here we offer and present unto
thee, O Lord, our selves, our souls and bodies, . . ."

However briefly, we need to see how powerful an image
of the person and personal relations can be as against the
pale, weak force of argument. People can think and say they
believe one thing, while their lives are actually controlled by
something else.

No Christian theology does or can do other than set out the
primacy of love in the life of persons. Love is not a theological
argument. It is not even a sentiment. It is a way of being
related to other people and of shaping the self to that relation. The sentiment we call love is delight and reward, so it
is a rightful part of love. The theological argument about love
is a protection against the intrusion of other ideas; it is
pedagogy, it is explanation, it is several other things, all
proper and necessary, as long as we know that love is a thing
done, and neither sentiment nor argument.

But, in displacing liturgy, argument turned the whole
thing on its head. Argument came first, and the sentiment,
instructed by argument rather than act, lost its power to
control personality. Thus, in our culture and, God forgive us,
in our Churches, the truly dominant liturgical principle is not

love but competition, which is the very antithesis of love. It is not that the formative liturgy has disappeared, for human beings do not live without liturgy. It is rather that the liturgy has been displaced from the Church that surrendered it. The true American liturgy is the celebration of competition which is set out daily in liturgies of remarkable power and authority. There and not in the Church is where the person is truly formed. So distant is argument from the reality of our own lives that millions of people profess their belief in love with their mouths but are fundamentally shaped by the liturgies of competition, so corporate and national life are determined by that faith and not what we believe to be the true faith.

So much is part one of my argument. I have tried to set out several things by means of one illustrative case. First, personality as personhood is not something we possess whole and intact; it is something shaped by a liturgy, by some liturgy appearing somewhere. Second, there are always liturgies to shape personhood, since that is the only way the person is shaped. Third, it is the nature of liturgy to shape persons, not to illustrate argument and doctrine or to provide devotional sentiment.

I have also proposed a negative principle of great importance. The process of liturgical revision has done injury, not simply because it has concentrated so heavily on theological argument; theological argument is not in itself a bad thing. Rather the trouble comes from isolating one thing from another, treating the problem of children and the Eucharist as though it had no connection with the principle of Confirmation, treating Confirmation as a theological problem apart from anthropology and psychology. Theological argument is a legitimate and a necessary discipline. But its true life is found only in relation to and subordinate to the life of faith.

If, therefore, I have succeeded in defining the function of the liturgy and suggested certain ways of going about it as well as ways of not going about it, we must next look at the kind of person the liturgy shapes.

THE KIND OF PERSONALITY LITURGY SHAPES AND THE GENERAL CONFESSION

All personality is shaped by some ritual forces, but it *matters* what kind of personality is shaped. The role of the Christian liturgy is not psychological therepeutics and reconstruction apart from a model of the person; the role of the Christian liturgy is to shape the person to the true model of the Christian life.

One test case must stand for the whole. If I choose the Prayer of General Confession for my example, I am not saying that the Christian life is basically sinful or the acknowledgment of sin. Rather, again, this test case demonstrates the way things should not be done and an indispensable precondition for doing things right.

First, let us look at the principal clause in the revised prayer: "We have not loved you with our whole heart; we have not loved our neighbors as ourselves."

On the face of it, the clause is literally true, and therefore unexceptional. But the trouble with assertions is that they usually contain more than they seem to contain, and this assertion contains a hidden positive. It is saying that we have, in fact, loved God and loved our neighbor, even though not as much as we should. This is not true.

I was talking to a young curate about this passage, commenting that I deplored the weakening of the sense of sin. He replied, "We ought not to appeal to people through fear."

This is, again, the kind of problem theological argument gets into. In the interests of one part of an argument, the rest is neglected. There is no great problem reconstructing the logic. Love is good; fear is bad. Fear inhibits and falsifies love. Thinking about sin nourishes fear. Therefore, we must play down the idea of sin.

Unfortunately, logic of this kind has little to do with reality. I am faced with a lion and afraid. There are a number of things you might tell me. The lion might be old and decrepit and unable to hurt a child. I might not have noticed that I was protected from the lion by a strong, nearly invisible glass. But don't tell me that fear is a debilitating neurosis that is bad for me when I am confronted with a young healthy, hungry lion. The question about fear is not whether it is good or bad but whether there is reason for it.

The question is whether there is something for us to fear. The atheists are not afraid of an angry god, but presumably we, at least, can set that argument aside. We might try to convince ourselves that God doesn't care about our sin, but that is a little hard to do. The revision chose another course —that we really haven't sinned very much or very significantly. We are good, but a little—just a little—less good than we ought to be. The guide book to the proposed Prayer Book sums up this point of view in two sentences I would not have dared write as caricature:

The tone of the resulting liturgies corresponded to a deepseated need of late medieval and post medieval psyches. There seems little doubt, however, that the language strikes many serious Christians of the twentieth century as exaggerated. (Prayer Book Studies 29 Revised, The Church Hymnal Corporation, 1976, p. 41.)

We are not in the realm of debate but in the realm of empirical observation. What, in fact, is our character as a people?

How, in the name of God, can we, living in one of the cruelest and bloodiest centuries of human history, speak so lightly of sin? Within the memory of most of us, Jews by the hundreds of thousands, by the millions, were slaughtered, starved, tortured, degraded. Seek the record for the Christian protests against this infamy. See, with pain, how few there were. Then ask if we truly love our fellow human beings. This was not done by people "over there." Germany, too, was a "Christian" nation. Shiploads of Jews were turned away from our ports, and *Guatemala* received more refugees than we did. Our own Air Force had the Norden bomb sight, an instrument of extraordinary precision. The location of the death camps was known. Not once was one attacked. Not once were the gates blown open or the gas chambers bombed.

Is this history the act of isolated wicked people who do not represent us all? Look again at the true history of our country. From the northeast, from the central east, from the southeast, from the south, from the southwest, our people came, cross in one hand and gun in the other, and in one of the cruelest campaigns of slaughter in history murdered Indians by the hundreds of thousands. Was the true voice of the Church the few who protested? Or was it Colonel Coddington, who said at the Sand Creek Massacre about the children: "Kill them all. Nits grow up into lice"?

A few decades later, this red tide of murder leaped the Pacific Ocean and fell with murderous fury on three tiny nations in Southeast Asia and for ten horrible years killed them, raped them, abused them, degraded them, ending in a cataclysm of deadly rage with no sense and no purpose other than the killing itself.

What was the voice of the Christian Church during this holocaust? There were, indeed, a few voices raised. We can take a melancholy pride in the fact that, when the police of the tyrant hunted the Jesuit, Daniel Berrigan, they finally found him at the home of one of our own people, William Stringfellow. But remember, too, that the same man who gave haven to the Jesuit also wrote the book, *My People Is the Enemy.* Unfortunately, Daniel Berrigan was not the voice of the Church. The voice of the Church was the Protestant evangelist and the Catholic cardinal who blessed both the killers and the killing.

Have we succeeded in pushing even this infamy into the past? Remember this: The two great buildings of our Church are in New York and Washington. Those two cities contain some of the most monstrous slums ever made by man. In those slums the human body and the human spirit are oppressed as they are in few places on earth. There is filth, hunger, degradation, murder, rape, torture, whoredoms. Those two Churches possess such wealth and control, such power as the human mind cannot imagine. If representatives of either of those institutions are wryly aware that they don't even have the funds to maintain the buildings, let me remind them that they are not the Church. The people is the Church; and, since the Episcopal Church, in its harmlessness, has a special attraction for the wealthy and the powerful, the wealth and the power are in the people. If you combine their wealth and their power with that of the other Churches—we are, after all, a "Christian" country—the wealth and the power are beyond comprehension. There is enough to abolish the slums. But the slums are still there. And will be there tomorrow. And will be there next year. And will be there ten years from now. And the slums in Chapel Hill, North Carolina, will be there. And I will make speeches like this. And go home and do nothing else.

We have done those things which we ought not to have done. We have left undone those things which we ought to have done.

The words of a true liturgy have strange effects on us. I used to be required to say, "The burden of my sin is intolerable to me." Now, this is a strange statement. In truth, it ought to say, "I think the burden of my sins ought to be intolerable to me." Or "I ought to be bothered about them more than I am." Or, like the new prayer, "I have a small burden of sin; its not very big and it's getting smaller so I won't bother very much about it." But it says none of those things. It says the burden of my sins is intolerable to me. Now, the truth of the matter is that the burden of my sins doesn't bother me at all. So the Church has made me lie. And *that* bothers me. I am, as the revised prayer would have it, a moderately truthful man. But outright lying troubles me, and I begin to think about it. So I look closer, and I don't much like what I see. I look closer at the Christian Church, and I don't much like what I see there either, for the Christian Church, in the name of the love of God in Christ, has caused more human suffering than any institution in human history.

We are, then, in sin. We are sinners; and if we claim other-
wise or slight our sin, then we have lied. This is not a lie that
heals as the other one might where I am measured against
what I ought to be, but a lie that hides from us what we really
are. It is a lie that kills and does not raise up, that wounds and
does not heal, that conceals and does not uncover.

What is the significance of our sinfulness for the liturgy?

It is the function of the liturgy to take the corrupted and
transform it into the image of the uncorrupted. As long as we
are false to ourselves, as long as we deny what we are and
have done, as long as we are so easily and casually satisfied
with what we are, then that long we are in our sin and
unavailable for change. It is the function of the liturgy, not
to judge us but to hold before us the model by which we are
compelled to judge ourselves. It is the function of the liturgy
to compel us by word, by repetitions, by rhythm, by the
dynamics of our body, to shape our imagination to the body
of the Lord, so that when we leave the service we carry some
nourishment with us that might sustain us in our falsehood
until we return to it and are shaped again and go out and
back and, in the rhythm of worship and work, discipline our
souls to the image of the Lord.

The issue is not the modesty of private devotion but life
itself. It is one of the terrible truths of human experience that
without death there is no life, that life is only the other side
of death. To deny death is to deny life—and the denial of life
is death. It is not accidental that one of the prime symbols of
our day, one of the causes now intruding into the sanctuary
itself, is precisely the idolatry of death and unfruitfulness.

Who then, will deliver us from the body of this death?

I have completed two of my three parts and come now to
the third. First, let me sum up where we are, not following
the same order.

1. People are not complete and ready-made persons who
do or don't do things like liturgies. Who they are is formed
by a liturgy, some liturgy. Insofar as the world is secular, the
people are not formed at all; they wander vaguely without

hope and direction. But it is not a secular world. There are religions aplenty to take over the task we have abandoned.

2. It is the function of the Christian liturgy to hold before us the truth of who we are—the whole, remorseless truth—hold it before us, not in judgment but in the hope that we will measure ourselves against it and make our own judgment and, out of that judgment, make a true confession.

Confession, full and complete, is an absolute condition. We do not traffic in comfort for the mildly uncomfortable middle class. The issue is life and death—or a death raised to life.

3. This self, once known in and by the liturgy, is lifted up and laid on the altar, a true sacrifice, broken and contrite. *Then,* and not until then, can it be remade, returned in the elements, now the meal that nourishes the newborn soul.

4. Once received reborn, the soul rejoices in the Great Thanksgiving. If I am only modestly bad, I rejoice and give thanks with equal modesty for a deliverance I didn't very much need. The Great Thanksgiving is the response to a great deliverance.

THE POWER OF HUMANNESS AND THE ORDINATION OF WOMEN

I am going to say very little about the ordination of women as such. That issue, happily, is settled. What I want to do with the ordination of women is to talk about the opportunity it presents for the recovery of what we are about to lose.

Thus I have tried to set out what liturgy is. Liturgy is not a devotional exercise. It is not a theological argument. It is, it must be, the power that nourishes life. We can achieve that power not by argument or politics but only if we are open to the *whole* force of life and of death. And this is the significance of the ordination of women for the revision of the liturgy.

I do not propose that women are any closer to the forces of life than are men; I certainly do not propose that women are wiser and better than men. For what we have learned is that women are people with about the same proportion of wisdom and stupidity, strength and weakness as men. I am not, at the moment, talking about the significance of *women* for the liturgy. Rather it is their ordination, the placing of women at the central action of the liturgy, that is so significant.

What this does is place sex at the center of our liturgical action. Despite its use as a euphemism for coitus, sex refers to gender. What the ordination of women has done, therefore, is place at the center of the liturgy the assertion that we are men and we are women.

This the Church has not done for a very long time. In fact, the Church has carefully avoided doing that throughout most of its life. We had better find out why.

The two most powerful forces in the life of every human being are economics and sex. This is as it must be; the one is the sustenance of our life, the other is the perpetuation of it. So the problem is not their centrality but what we do with them. Our resolution of the problem of economics and sex shapes everything else we do and so defines our selves.

In the past, almost universally, the role of women was central to the religious imagination, so central that the force of sexual attraction and fertility embodied in women was commonly considered a divine force, certainly a sacred power that was of central importance to religion.

One thing we know little about is the psychic life of other people, particularly those in the distant past. We don't know and can't know what this did to the actual women who had to bear so heavy a load of mythological significance. We suspect it did them little good. Again, there is great variation from one culture to another but there are not many which place women in general in a place of equality.

The Church did not set itself to be antisexual, as ill-informed history would have it. The crucial definition was the clear and unequivocal statement: In Christ there is no male and female (Galatians 3:28). Clearly, without doubt, the Church was asserting that women are first of all (or perhaps finally of all) persons to be dealt with as such.

The Church took nearly two thousand years to make any sense out of this principle and during that time has badly abused it. Christendom has managed to suppress women as badly as any society and, even worse, interpreted the definition as somehow meaning that the gender of women is wicked and that the sexual relation is evil.

But we are, incorrigibly, male and female. In Christ there is no male and female, for the body of Christ is androgyne, containing both. But we live under the conditions of this earth, and on this earth we are male and female, powerfully drawn to each other. Out of this struggle, the struggle between our natural sexuality and the attempt to go beyond it or deny it, there has grown the strains and tensions, the perversities, the neuroses, that accompanied a distorted sexuality.

We are a stupid race and learn very slowly. The price has been high, but something has been bought with the price if we will only see it through the fog of ignorance and prejudice that is being thrown up around it. What we have bought is the equality of women and all the opportunities that equality brings.

There is, in the human economy, no gain without a dreadful price in human suffering; there is no opportunity without dangers, and dangers there are aplenty in this situation. There is the danger of again denying women's sexuality in the achievement of equality. There is the terrible danger of denying the fruitfulness in order to secure equality. There is the danger for the Church that it revert to the cults that all biblical religions fought against. All of these are clear and present dangers, passionately advocated by some in the Church.

I will make a claim that is wholly undemonstrable: without the proper liturgy of the Church, the gains will be lost. The defense of those gains is undertaken now with politics and reason, and politics and reason will prove woefully inadequate. However faithless Christendom has been to one of its basic principles, it was that principle, carefully nurtured, that brought what we now have. It is only as the Church meets its great responsibility that the achievement can be protected. In the ancient rituals, the goddess and the priestess were embodied functions. In the Church, despite the ugly misogyny of Origen and Tertullian and their successors, it was declared that women are persons. Because we are ugly and limited, the sexuality of women was denied and profaned, but the affirmation was maintained. Now, if we have the will and the courage, sexuality can return and with it the wholeness of the human.

Thus, the ordination of women has consequences and also gives us an opprotunity; that opportunity is a necessity for the common health. While the consequences are varied, the most important consequence is precisely at the point of the liturgy.

Now it may be evident why I began as I did. Liturgy is neither argument nor devotion. Argument is a framework of liturgy or an explanatory consequence, but it is not liturgy; and it is not the function of the liturgy to set out argument. Devotion is an accompaniment of liturgy; it is a result of the liturgy, and one of our greatest failures is the lack of a disciplined devotional life to continue the work of the liturgy. But liturgy is not devotion.

Liturgy is a dramatic action that shapes the worshiper to the model of the Christian life. Now, at long last, we have placed our twofold humanness at the center of our liturgy and, with that humanness, all the energies of the human.

I spoke earlier of the androgynous nature of the Body of Christ. To affirm and sustain its nature, the Church has chosen to suppress the sexuality of its priesthood. To the extent that the great communions focus their life on the liturgy, the priest suppresses his masculinity in an androgynous role. With some Churches it goes so far as to deny priests all manifestation of their masculinity by requiring celibacy. In lesser cases, it is denial only in the sacerdotal role, when they are vested in the silks, brocades, and laces of the garments of women.

It might be that women priests could be amalgamated to

this androgynous role. I do not believe it humanly possible; too great an energy of the human imagination is focused on the concrete reality of the priest. Neither do I believe it required of us, for we are at one of those great turning points when we can begin to incorporate one of our great truths into the common life.

I do not see this as possible with the new Prayer Book. It was not possible with the old one either, but that one had a different function, now accomplished. It is not possible with the new one primarily because of its sentimentalizing the idea of our sinfulness.

This does not suggest that women in the priesthood increase the opportunity for sinfulness. I am rather talking about the reality of our humanness.

It is sentimental to call sex sinful. It is equally sentimental to call it beautiful. It *is* part of who we are. Every person in the Church has been conceived in the same way, by an occasion that may have been ugly, may have been boring, may have been passionately delightful with all the mess and comic acrobatics involved. Every one of us grew in a sack buried among the intestines and was born between faeces and urine. This shocked the Fathers but it should not. It is a condition of being human.

The great experiment of the Church for a time suppressed the passion and pain of sexuality. It burst out in a variety of ways or turned inward and rotted. It often emerged into the marvelous flower of the Church's art and music, that mode of theology which the dogmatic officers of the Church have never brought under control. But it has no part in the formal life or liturgy of the Church.

That option is no longer available. The weakening of the Church's authority—partly because it could not forever suppress so great a human energy—meant that the great experiment was over; and natural sexuality, tainted by the false erotics of commercial culture, is breaking out everywhere.

Not being any longer conscious of the meaning of the great experiment, the Church is helpless to resist the onslaught.

The onslaught becomes explicit in the passionate proclamation of the primacy of sexuality in the characteristic forms of gratified indulgence, unfruitfulness, and death. That will not do. That is no more than one of the forms of modern apostasy.

The ordination of women places the danger squarely in the center of our corporate life, not because women are more sexual than men but because their presence places sexuality at the center of our corporate life. One consequence of this act is to give us an opportunity to recover again the place we have lost by compelling us to recover a true liturgy.

Thus the argument reaches an appropriate point for summary in order to see how the denial of womanliness requires or compels the denial of sin. Ultimately both stem from a deep fear of life and the forces of life. Sin is an inescapable dimension of mortality, a consequence of our finitude and humanness. Since we refuse to face the reality of sin and its deadly consequences, it is essential to deny the burgeoning fruitfulness of life. To deny fruitfulness, it is necessary to deny the womanliness of women and to idolize death and unfruitfulness. Yet it is precisely the function of the liturgy to take up the wholeness of life, including its sin and its fruitfulness, and shape it to the model of the Christian life.

Thus the consequences that became the opportunity now become the measure: our liturgy will be reformed only when it can take up this great energy into the life of faith and shape it to the model of the true and loving life.

The opportunity and the measure become the means. When we realize that liturgy is not devotion or theology but the controlling shape of the basic human energies, then we can know better how to do it, for only as the energies are admitted, not denied, will the liturgy respond to its required shape.

This does not mean that any part of the language of sexuality should enter the liturgy. That would be apostasy in its purest form. Rather the liturgy must be so great a shape of energy that it can take into itself all the powerful, dangerous human energies and reshape them to the sacred image. The

liturgy is neither devotion nor argument but drama, enactment, reenactment, a re-calling of the Christ whose presence
can take up the wholeness of the human into himself.

This is the meaning of the great prayer: "Here we offer and
present unto thee, . . . our selves, our souls and bodies to be
a reasonable, holy, and living sacrifice unto thee; . . ." The
Eucharist is not a refreshing meal. It is the Eucharist, the
great rejoicing, only if it is first the sacrifice, when we are
compelled against our selfish wills to offer up our whole
selves to be remade into the image of Christ and given back
to us in the elements of the body of Christ.

It must be truly an enactment, an action that involves the
whole self. This involves us in a redefinition of the priesthood
which can liberate us from much superstition. The priest is
neither our father nor our mother, however much loving
care goes into the role of pastor. Neither can the priest make
that ultimate claim of arrogance, to be or even to represent
the Christ. The priest is the representative of our humanity,
now happily the whole of our varied humanity, as leader and
spokesman.

But the liturgy is not a spectator sport. It is a drama whose
audience is God and not the people. The people are not
spectators but actors, and it is their enactment, with their
appointed representative, that re-calls, makes present, the
Christ who receives the sacrifice. Only so can the sacrifice be
truly offered. Only as the drama is enacted by the whole self,
by the body and the mind, by ideas and rhythms, by act and
feeling, can there be a self to be offered to be received back
as a soul.

7

THE ECUMENICAL CONTEXT
OF THE PROPOSED BOOK

Horace T. Allen, Jr.

EDITOR'S INTRODUCTION

Horace Allen is an ordained minister in the Presbyterian Church and has served as Director of the Office of Worship and Music for two Presbyterian denominations. In his essay, Allen gives some perspective to the Proposed Episcopal Prayer Book by indicating the liturgical work of other denominations during the last ten years. He makes a strong case for his thesis that there is a growing consensus among denominations, and he identifies what these areas of common direction are. Then, he mentions several unresolved issues on which denominations are still working. Finally, he issues an appeal that Episcopalians be attentive to the contributions of other Christian bodies and maintain our purpose as a bridge. This essay is based upon an article published in the Union Seminary Quarterly Review *(Volume 31, No. 3, Spring 1976, pp. 155–168) entitled, "Is There an Emerging Consensus Concerning the Liturgy?"*

My principle theme is to describe what I take to be an impressive emerging ecumenical consensus concerning the liturgy of the Western Church. It is my thesis that it has been the wisdom and economy of the Holy Spirit to encourage what has become known as the Ecumenical Movement, in both its organized and unorganized forms, not principally to unite vast denominations or even to create interdenominational bureaucracies but rather to create the kind of conversations among the Churches in matters liturgical which would open up a much truer and swifter way to unity: namely, unity in Word and Sacrament. It is my growing suspicion and hope that one bright Sunday morning we are all going to wake up to realize that we are all doing the same thing: singing the same hymns, reading the same lections, celebrating the same calendar, performing rites of marked structural similarity, perhaps preaching sermons crafted in common. The question will then be, Why are we doing all that in all those separate and expensive buildings?

So now let me gather together some data, from my own Presbyterian and ecumenical experience of the last several years, to provide some substantiation for such a thesis, suspicion, and hope. I am going to sketch what I take to be four dimensions of an emerging liturgical consensus, then identify a number of open issues, and finally issue to Episcopalians something of an appeal for our immediate and interrelated future.

THE EMERGING CONSENSUS

First, let us look at the emerging pattern of the principal service for Sunday morning. I center in the Lord's Day, because it is in terms of that worship pattern that most Christians identify themselves denominationally. For most people, to be an Episcopalian or a Presbyterian or a Methodist means to do this or that distinctive thing during the Sunday assembly. It is therefore more than significant that the Sunday service has been the subject of considerable activity in practically every major denomination these last ten years. This era has very recently been given first-rate documentation in a splendid book by the Methodist, Professor James White, entitled *Christian Worship in Transition* (Abingdon, 1976), which I cannot too highly recommend.

In the last ten years every tradition in this country that has anything like a rite or even the outline of a rite has produced a new pattern or a revised pattern or language for that structure. The Presbyterians, North and South; the Lutherans, four major groups; the United Methodists; the United Church of Christ; the Consultation on Church Union—to say nothing of the Episcopal Church and, of course, the Roman Catholic Church—all have in the last ten years produced new rites. Were I to bind all those rites in brown paper and put them on a table, you would probably have some difficulty in sorting them out as to denominational origin. They are astonishingly similar in conception.

In the first place, they are all in modern English. Only Episcopalians have maintained the older English as an option. My assumption is that there is a very good reason for that, aside from the well-known Anglican virtue of finding a happy compromise in a difficult situation. After all, the Anglican Church is the only Western Church to have put the whole thing into the vernacular, word for word. The Lutherans did it bit by bit. Calvinists tried it but lost practically all fixed texts by the time of the Westminster Assembly in the late seventeenth century. The Methodists fairly rapidly jettisoned Wesley's version of Anglican rites. The Free Churches never bothered with rites. And Rome stuck to Latin. Only Anglicans attempted the Reformation liturgical program in its totality, at the linguistic point. In my estimation, that is much of your present trauma now and the underlying reason for Rites One and Two.

Another aspect of these recent rites for Sunday is that they all assume a threefold pattern of (1) entry, (2) liturgy of the Word and (3) Sacrament or other response. Thus, this emerging consensus is in fact Ante-Communion. This must be some kind of progress after centuries of *anti*-Communion, manifested in the Protestant preaching service or Morning Prayer and sermon.

The content of these three substructures is also remarkably

similar. The entry rite generally includes praise, which is possibly a psalm, some kind of movement or procession at the same time or just before, and perhaps an act of confession. Only we Presbyterians still feel obligated to require confession every Sunday at the outset of worship; that's not because we're such terrible sinners but that we're so guilty as a matter of principle.

The liturgy of the Word in all these rites includes both Old and New Testament lessons with psalmody intervening in the form of responsory psalms, hymns, anthems, or responsive reading. There then follows the sermon, which conjunction is itself an important advance upon the more recent tradition of separating Scripture and preaching by all manner of liturgical and nonliturgical distractions. Finally, there is some creedal response to the Word.

The transition to the sacramental service is made by such acts as intercessory prayer, sharing of concerns, offering, and the exchange of Peace. If the Eucharist is not to be celebrated, a general thanksgiving may be made followed by singing and the blessing.

There is a structure, which in its ecumenical acceptance, is impressive.

A second common dimension to be discovered in these rites lies in their assumptions concerning their social/temporal context. Naturally, there is only so much a liturgical text can do toward determining such matters, but they do what they can.

On the one hand, these texts deliberately introduce into the worship of the Church as much of the human, social, and secular life of the people of God as is possible. They all include moments wherein clergy and laity are urged to introduce personal and contemporary concerns, feelings, and needs. It is interesting to note that that most ancient of Christian rites, the Liturgy of St. John Chrysostom, begins at just such a place. The first fully corporate moment is the great Litany of Peace, whose response *Kyrie eleison* is the origin of the first prayer of the Western Mass. That litany is basically

an intercession for peace, salvation, the Church and her ministers, public servants and the government, the region, good
crops and favorable weather, travelers, the sick, the suffering, prisoners, and personal deliverance from evil and danger. The Liturgy of St. John Chrysostom begins where people
live. Modern rites are restoring that relevance.

On the other hand, these rites also assume a temporal
context which is not only the time in which people live but
the time in which the Church lives, the Christian Year. Every
one of these new texts is trying hard to reintroduce the Christological simplicity and power of the classic Christian calendar. Remember that the Christian Year at the time of the
sixteenth-century Reformation was a terrible mess in which
the centrality of Christmas, Easter, and Pentecost had been
all but lost in a complicated confusion of theological feasts,
the Marian cycle, saints days, and local commemorations.
Rome is at last "cleaning house," and Protestantism is recovering the centralities. Episcopalians, and perhaps the Lutherans, did a clean job without throwing out the baby with the
bath water.

All these new rites assume the classic Christian Year, complete with a system of propers: psalms, readings, and collects.
Not only that, but the proper pericopes are now a shared
treasure. The three-year lectionary which was produced by
the Roman Catholic Church has now been taken over, with
adaptations, by Episcopalians, Lutherans, Methodists, Presbyterians, and the Consultation on Church Union.

To my biblical imagination, this growing use of a common
lectionary may be one of the most important ecumenical
steps of all. The power of such an agreement is considerable.
Already, all over the country there are study groups of pastors, priests, and ministers, who work over the lections each
week. Sooner or later they'll probably start exchanging pulpits from time to time. And where will it all end? Let's hope
it doesn't. Some of us have believed for a long time that the
true and lasting unity of the Church catholic will grow only
out of fellowship about the Word. At this rate, *communio in*

sacris, even with Rome, may not be as far away as most of us probably think.

A third dimension to this emerging set of liturgical assumptions is the matter and the manner of participation. To paraphrase (and distort) a very great hymn, one of the effects of the current liturgical movement is to transform our congregations from "ye watchers" into "ye holy ones." We've had watchers galore for too long. As one of my former colleagues in West Virginia used to say, "What Christians do after church is to go home and have fried preacher and chicken for dinner." That is to say, our people's only relationship to worship has been that of the critic; they were more "watchers" (spectators) than "holy ones" (participants). These new rites assume a vastly increased level of participation and in a number of ways.

Primarily, and this is not a function of the rites themselves but of the way in which they are being prepared and introduced, there is the assumption that Sunday's assembly will be planned and produced by a much more democratic and less clerical or professional instrumentality. Oddly enough, this is happening much more seriously and extensively among Roman Catholic churches than among ourselves. Yet, this must be at least part of the Reformation conviction about shared priesthood and baptismal birthright.

Participation is being encouraged not only by singing and speaking but also by the careful use of silence and other sensual means of communication. Churches which heretofore have avoided visual symbolism and vestments are becoming more alert through the use of banners, visual projections, and vestments. Thus the alb and stole as the clergy's usual vestment seems to be emerging as yet another aspect of consensus.

A further and very important means of participation which the new rites tend to assume is that we will find ways to be informal with each other as well as formal. Spontaneity, not as an end in itself but as a means of participation, is finding its way back even into Presbyterian and Episcopalian worship. This is no more sorely needed than in those central liturgical acts, the sacraments. We Presbyterians have made such a formal, solemn thing of the Lord's Supper that our new invitation—"Friends: this is the joyful feast of the people of God"—must strike children and casual onlookers as some sort of joke. And how has it ever come about that in Baptism, the sacrament of initiation, the initiates, if they be infants, are basically unwelcome at their own welcoming? We can't wait to get them out so that we can go on with the "usual thing." Only some self-conscious and serious informality will be able to save us from these deformities of the sacraments and of worship in general. At this point we probably have much to learn from the Roman Catholics, the Orthodox, *and* the Methodists.

The final dimension to which I wish to allude, and I do it only fleetingly, is the return of the ancient assumption that the weekly liturgy is the primary place in the congregation's life of both pastoral and catechetical life. Pastoral calls and Sunday Church Schools are both, in the long history of the Church, recent innovations. The community in its assembly and mutual edification (to use St. Paul's term for what we call "worship") has traditionally been the place of continuing catechesis and pastoral care. To depend primarily on the clergy for both or either is to participate in the deformation of the people of God. Precisely that sort of deformation lurks behind our clericalized liturgies, failing Sunday Schools, and overburdened pastor-counselors. We seem to be returning to a sense of the gathered community as the only possible place for nurture in the faith. The fascinating writings of Professor John Westerhoff of Duke Divinity School amply document this dimension, at least in its educative aspect.

UNRESOLVED PROBLEMS

I would like to turn to the matter of what seem to be the most extensive areas of continuing discussion and reform. It is the case that most of us are also working furiously at the same unresolved problems.

The first is initiation. Roman Catholics are in considerable agreement that their new rites for the initiation of adults have opened up an unexpected Pandora's Box of issues involving infant Baptism, the character of the congregation as community, and even the restoration of the catechumenate. Across the way, both large Presbyterian Churches are struggling with their discipline of admission to Holy Communion (Baptized or not? Confirmed or not?), the relation of Baptism to Holy Communion, the role of the congregation's Ruling Eldership in such discipline, and continuing indecision about the age for Baptism. Lutherans are revising their initiation process to deal with the increasingly obvious ambiguity of the meaning of Confirmation. And Episcopalians are having their own difficulties, which are not made simpler by virtue of the fact that the bishop has been identified with a major step in that initiation process.

I strongly suspect that we shall all begin to find a way out of these problems, both theologically and liturgically, when we learn to think about sacraments not so much in terms of "who gets what and how?" (which puts all the emphasis on the recipient and his or her age/faith state) but on "who does what and why?" (which shifts the center of the discussion to the congregation-community). If you want some good reading along that line, I would send you back to Dietrich Bonhoeffer who, thirty years ago in *The Cost of Discipleship* (Macmillan, 1963), said about Baptism, "The problem is not whether infant baptism is baptism at all, but that the final and unrepeatable character of infant baptism necessitates certain restrictions in its use . . . it must be insisted that the sacrament should be administered only where there is a firm faith present which remembers Christ's deed of salvation wrought for us once and for all. That can only happen in a living Christian community" (p. 261). If Baptism doesn't "work," as people casually suggest, it can only be confessed that the cause is the absence of the community of faith as catechist, pastor, and family.

I'd also like to add to that witness just a bit of wit and wisdom from the East on the question of initiation, if only to suggest what an important business the Sunday event is. I recall a very luminous moment at Union Seminary in New York when the distinguished Orthodox scholar Father John Meyendorff was lecturing on initiation and made the obvious point that the Orthodox Churches have never separated Baptism, Confirmation, and first Communion but administer them as one rite to infants or adults. One rather naïve student asked him, "Well, Father Meyendorff, in that case, when and how does the Orthodox Church do what the Churches of the West do in their rites of adolescent Confirmation?" After a brief pause, the answer was forthcoming, with that characteristic Orthodox certainty, and with surprise that the question would even be put: "Every Sunday at the Liturgy."

We're all working away at the question of initiation. The universal upsurge of interest in renewal rites and the great Vigil of Easter are part and parcel of this issue.

The second open issue is predictable: the other dominical sacrament, the Lord's Supper. The issue is put nicely in the essay by Professor Dixon who describes it as "meal and sacrifice." Among more Protestant bodies, the same dichotomy is expressed as Eucharist or *Agapé*. Indeed, our new Presbyterian *Worshipbook* includes an order for an *Agapé* which is introduced as "a fellowship meal that should not be confused with the Lord's Supper." To any student of early Church history or commentator on the present scene, that may sound slightly ludicrous as well as futile. In a broader sense, this same worry is giving rise to fears that contemporary worship is abandoning the vertical for the horizontal, of becoming, in George MacLeod's phrase, "All-matey with the Almighty." Once again, Dietrich Bonhoeffer may be the most contemporary theologian around, as he spoke in one of his later letters from prison of "the transcendence of the other." And when it comes to the seeming contradiction of having a sacred meal, a sacrificial meal, do we not all need to recover our Hebraic subconsciousness wherein there is no such thing as a secular meal?

A third developing issue involves the twin matters of reconciliation and the Peace. We are all experiencing extraordinary resistance to the exchange of the Peace, and at least the Roman Catholic Church is worrying considerably about reconciliation-confession. Perhaps much of the trouble at this point is failure to realize the relation between these two events in the life of the Church. The Peace is not, as is so often the case, a bit of "ecclesiastical post office" (in the phrase of Paul Lehmann, lately of Union Seminary) or American chumminess; it is at its heart a discreet sign of the basically corporate character of sin and the churchly character of forgiveness. Both Catholicism and Protestantism individualized this business of reconciliation and only now in the context of new liturgical possibilities are reintroducing it into the gathered life of the congregation. Until that is fully realized, the Peace will come off at best as "loving those who love you"; or, at worst, as a resented intrusion into the solemnities of the worship of Almighty God. Further, with no genuine reconciliation, our liturgical occasions will continue to be tragically sad confirmations of individuals in their guilt that they are not doing enough, believing enough, or giving enough.

A fourth common problem we are all having is the problem of the Psalter. In one generation we have all lost both our texts and our tunes. The Roman Catholics lost Latin and then Gregorian, Presbyterians have lost the Scottish Psalter with its metrical tunes, Episcopalians are trying to decide whether Anglican chant can handle the new translations, and the Lutherans are teaching themselves a system of inflected speech. And every time there is a new translation of the Bible, there is a new Psalter; and all the translations are "discriminatory" in their language.

This is no minor crisis. For most of the Church's life, the Psalter was its prayer book and its hymn book. Indeed, the distinction was unknown. If the Psalms are not the heart of Christian prayer and praise, we're all in trouble. Getting them back on the hearts and lips of Christian people is a first priority of the liturgical movement.

Fifthly, as a kind of continuing common problem about the liturgy, we are all trying to find a balance between structure and freedom, cult and culture, closed and open assemblies. If that sounds like far too an imposing an agenda for anyone, I would like to leave you—as Presbyterians tend to do—with St. Paul. That finest and early liturgist gave the Church one of its most comprehensive liturgical treatises in I Corinthians 11–15. No, those chapters do not comprise a prayerbook. They are the effort of a practicing pastor struggling with a missionary congregation to hold together structure and freedom, in word and sacrament, for an event that was both open and closed. At issue were cultural differences of gender and economics and cultic differences of a diversity of gifts. Religious exhibitionism and personal greediness conspired to upset the delicate balance which must exist in any community between individual needs and corporate realities. Freedom and structure, which in St. Paul's mind were not opposites but complementary, had come into conflict. His appeal in Chapter 13, therefore, is to the highest of virtues, love. For that profound liturgist, love was the secret of good liturgy. We have yet to approach that sensitivity in our liturgical renewal.

AN APPEAL FOR THE FUTURE

In conclusion I should like to issue something of an appeal to my friends and colleagues of the Episcopal Church. The first is that you be attentive to the renaissance in Rome. I am fully aware of all the voices within and without the Roman Church which are decrying the shambles of the "new Mass," contemporary language texts, and the like. Remember, however, that the Roman Church thinks in much longer terms than we do, and she has been counted down and out before —by us! No less serious a critic of the Church of Rome than Karl Barth has put the question this way: "What if one day Rome (without ceasing to be Rome) simply overtakes us in the question of the renewal of the church on the basis of the word and the spirit of the gospel, and puts us in the shade?"

(Eberhard Busch, *Karl Barth*, Fortress Press, 1976, p. 481)

Secondly, be at least as attentive to the possibility of a liturgically emergent East. The Orthodox Churches have yet to be heard from at the point of liturgical renewal. Their caution is puzzling in Western eyes, but it may have its profound reasons. The vernacular is beginning to be used; such is the case in the Russian Orthodox seminary, St. Vladimir's. Certain small congregations around the country, made up not of ethnic but of converted Orthodox are doing the same. If a genuine dialogue can get going with the East, we may find that we have considerably more to deal with than we ever dreamed.

Thirdly, I would like to pray you to be alert and receptive even to the possibilities of Protestantism. Our seriousness about sermons is not exactly a vice, and Episcopalians have known that intensity about hearing the Word in the long and great tradition of celebrating the Daily Offices. A liturgical expert, not commonly associated with the evangelical party of the Episcopal Church, commented to me that one of his concerns about the new Prayer Book is the possible "downgrading" of the Offices due to the book's Eucharistic centeredness. Do be attentive, not only to Protestantism's contemporary appropriation of so much that you have always taken for granted, but also to some of its own distinctive treasures—one of which is peculiarly that of that most impressive community, the Society of Friends: Silence.

Another preoccupation of Protestants may well be helpful to you: Its preoccupation with simplicity. One of the things which the Lord must be most nervous about is liturgical complexity. At that point, the professionals always take over. Another way of saying this is to caution you about the dangers of rubricism with the new, very comprehensive Book of Common Prayer. That is one of the blind alleys in which our Roman Catholic friends got trapped. For all our failures, we Protestants may have some wise warnings in this regard.

So, here endeth the lesson. It ends where you began, with being a bridge Church. The Episcopal Church has always prided itself on that, and well you might. A bridge's span, however, is ultimately dependent on the firmness with which the abutments are situated on either side of the river. And today the definition of which side is which is increasingly less clear. That doesn't make your ministry any easier. Finally, beware of books, for "the letter killeth but the Spirit giveth life" (II Corinthians 3:6).

BIBLIOGRAPHY

Annotated by William S. Pregnall

Associated Parishes, *The Great Vigil of Easter: A Commentary*. (Associated Parishes, Inc., P.O. Box 5562, Washington, D.C. 20016; 1977) A clear and concise commentary. Helpful reading before undertaking to do the service.

Associated Parishes, *The Holy Eucharist Rite Two: A Commentary*. (Associated Parishes, Inc., 1976) Excellent, simple resource on Rite II Eucharist.

Executive Council of the Episcopal Church, *Our Living Worship: A Study Guide for Liturgy*. (815 Second Avenue, New York, NY 10017; 1976) Also available on tape from Catacomb Cassettes, 404 National Bank of Georgia Building, 3376 Peachtree Road, N.E., Atlanta, GA 30326. Contributions from Ronald Miller, Michael Merriman, William Pregnall, Thomas Talley, and Leonel Mitchell.

Reginald H. Fuller, *Preaching the New Lectionary: The Word of God for the Church Today*. (The Liturgical Press, 1971) Although this commentary follows the Roman Catholic version of the lectionary, a good index makes it a valuable preaching resource.

Marion J. Hatchett, *A Manual of Ceremonial for the New Prayer Book*. (St. Luke's Bookstore, Sewanee, TN 37375; 1977) Recommendations of ceremonial to go with many of the liturgies in the new Prayer Book.

Marion J. Hatchett, *Sanctifying Life, Time, and Space: An Introduction to Liturgical Study*. (Seabury, 1976) An excellent compendium of liturgical data. Helps with historical and "why" questions.

Urban T. Holmes, *Confirmation: The Celebration of Maturity in Christ*. (Seabury, 1975) Discusses the changes in Christian initiation and presents a proposal to those who want to maintain an important place for Confirmation in parish life.

Urban T. Holmes, *Young Children and the Eucharist.* (Seabury, 1972) A rationale for Communion at an earlier age, with suggestions for parents and clergy on how to prepare children.

Robert W. Hovda, *Strong, Loving and Wise: Presiding in Liturgy.* (The Liturgical Conference, 1976) For clergy who want to get their liturgical style in line with the spirit of the Proposed Prayer Book.

Gabe Huck and Virginia Sloyan, editors, *Parishes and Families.* (The Liturgical Conference, 1973) Useful hints for parishes and families at every point in the Christian year. Useful for worship committees.

Liturgical Commission, Diocese of Virginia, "Guidelines for Christian Initiation." (Mimeographed, 1976) Available from the Diocesan Office, 110 West Franklin Street, Richmond, VA 23220) A good, brief, practical approach to Baptism, first Communion, and Confirmation

Marianne H. Micks, *The Future Present: The Phenonmenon of Christian Worship.* (Seabury, 1970) A profound look at some of the issues underlying all our revisions.

Leonel L. Mitchell, *Liturgical Change: How Much Do We Need?* (Seabury, 1975) Useful in helping people affirm change in liturgy.

Phillis Nobel, editor, *The Book of Bread.* (Seabury, 1975) All the recipes you'll need to vanquish the "wafer" from your church. This is a how to bake bread for the Eucharist book.

Donald Parsons, *The Holy Eucharist, Rite Two: A Devotional Commentary.* (Seabury, 1976) The Bishop of Quincy provides a guide to the devotional possibilities of Rite Two.

Gerard A. Pottebaum, *The Rites of People: Exploring the Ritual Character of Human Experience.* (The Liturgical Conference, 1975) It helps bridge the gap between ritual makers of the early Church and today's technological people as ritual makers.

William S. Pregnall, *Laity and Liturgy: A Handbook for Parish Worship.* (Seabury, 1975) A good introduction for lay persons to the notion of dramatic structure in the liturgy. A tool for people on worship committees.

Charles P. Price, *Introducing the Proposed Book.* Prayer Book Studies 29 Revised. (The Church Hymnal Corporation, 1976) The best, simple, one-volume introduction to the rationale and contents of the Proposed Prayer Book.

Proclamation: Aids for Interpreting the Lessons of the Church Year. (Fortress Press, 1973–1976) Eight separate booklets for each of cycles A, B, and C. Excellent brief commentaries for sermon preparation. Because of different authors, however, the quality varies from volume to volume.

Massey H. Shepherd, *The Psalms in Christian Worship: A Practical Guide.* (Augsburg, 1976) The title describes it.

Virginia Sloyan, editor, *Liturgy Committee Handbook: A Nine-Week Study Guide.* (The Liturgical Conference, 1971) Useful for new worship committees.

Daniel B. Stevick, *Holy Baptism.* Supplement to Prayer Book Studies 26. (The Church Hymnal Corporation, 1973) Although commenting on a service now revised, this is still the best brief discussion of the Baptism and Confirmation rites.

Daniel B. Stevick, *Language in Worship: Reflections on a Crisis.* (Seabury, 1970) Explains how the words we speak affect what happens to us in liturgical celebration.

William Sydnor, *Sunday's Scriptures: An Interpretation.* (Morehouse-Barlow, 1976) Useful for introducing the lessons or putting summary of them in bulletin.

James F. White, *Christian Worship in Transition.* (Abingdon, 1976) A survey of developments in Christian worship during the past decade by a Methodist professor of worship.

PERIODICALS

Liturgy. Bimonthly publication of the Liturgical Conference, 1221 Massachusetts Avenue, N.W., Washington, D.C. 20005. Subscription comes with annual membership fee of $25.00.

Open. The Journal of Associated Parishes, P.O. Box 5562, Washington, D.C. 20016. Subscription with annual membership fee of $15.00.

Worship. Published bimonthly by St. John's Abbey, Collegeville, MN 56321. $8.00 per year.